Skillful
Reading&Writing

Teacher's Book

3

Author: Stacey H. Hughes
Series Consultant: Dorothy E. Zemach

Macmillan Education
4 Crinan Street
London N1 9XW
A division of Macmillan Publishers Limited
Companies and representatives throughout the world

ISBN 978-0-230-43001-3

Text, design and illustration © Macmillan Publishers 2013
Written by Stacey H. Hughes

First published 2013

Note to Teachers

Designed by emc design limited

Cover design by emc design limited

Page layout by MPS Limited

The Academic Keyword List (AKL) was designed by Magali Paquot
at the Centre for English Corpus Linguistics, Université catholique de
Louvain (Belgium) within the framework of a research project led by
Professor Sylviane Granger.

http://www.uclouvain.be/en-372126.html

Author's acknowledgements

Many thanks to John, Juliet, and Sara for their support and
encouragement.

Please see Student's Book imprint page for visual walkthrough photo
credits. All author photos were kindly supplied by the authors.

The author(s) and publishers are grateful for permission to reprint the
following copyright material:

Material from *The Study Skills Handbook* by author Stella Cottrell,
copyright © Stella Cottrell 1999, 2003 & 2008, first published by
Palgrave Macmillan, reproduced with permission of the publisher.

Printed and bound in Thailand

2017 2016 2015 2014
10 9 8 7 6 5 4 3 2

Contents

Grammar	Writing skill	Writing task	Digibook video activity	Study skills
Clause joining with subordinators	Paragraph structure	A paragraph about your identity	Shared identity	Am I a smart reader?
Non-defining relative clauses	Transitions: introducing opposing ideas	The pros and cons of a design	The counterfeit wars	Editing and proofreading strategies
Adverb clauses of reason and purpose	Summarizing	A summary and a response paragraph	Thought development	Plagiarism
Adverbs as stance markers	Using sensory details in a narrative	Narrative essay: A time when you faced danger	Fire and fun	Managing stress
Object noun clauses with *that*	Using sentence variety	Response to an exam question	Our journey, our dreams	Strategies for writing timed essays
Passive modals: advice, ability, and possibility	Thesis statements	Persuasive essay: A health recommendation	Pills	Participating in online discussion boards
Unreal conditional in the past	Writing about cause and effect	Describing a challenging situation	Adaptation	Using desired outcomes to guide study strategy
Intensifier + comparative combinations	Effective hooks	A proposal	Profiles of success	Selecting and evaluating online sources
Cleft sentences with *what*	Using similes and metaphors	A descriptive anecdote	Communication	Using the thesaurus
The future progressive	Qualifying statistical data	A report on a current trend	Future friends	Developing a portfolio

VOCABULARY PREVIEW Pre-teaching essential vocabulary which appears in both texts within the unit.

BEFORE YOU READ These introductions to the reading topics prepare students for the upcoming subject matter.

GLOBAL READING Global reading is the first time the students will read the text; encouraging them to engage with the big issues and the overall picture.

CLOSE READING Following on from Global reading is Close reading. This is an in-depth detailed analysis of the text.

SKILLS BOXES These focus on the newly-presented skill, why it's important, and how to do it. They also highlight reading tips.

Vocabulary preview

Read the sentences. Then circle the word or phrase that is closest in meaning to the bold words.

1 Climbing Mount Everest was the greatest **achievement** of his life.
   a success   b fear
2 Julio's **ambition** is to become mayor of his city someday.
   a job   b goal
3 This team has the skill and **determination** to win the championship.
   a sense of humor   b strength of mind
4 If this **drought** continues, many farmers may go out of business.
   a cold weather   b dry weather
5 Top athletes must **endure** many hours of difficult training in all conditions.
   a continue through   b watch over
6 The desire to be accepted by our peers is **inherent** in all humans.
   a natural   b unusual
7 Janek has written **numerous** job applications, but so far without success.
   a a few   b many
8 A large **proportion** of high school students feel some stress about the future.
   a size   b percentage

READING 1   Making a difference

Before you read

Work with a partner. Think of an experience when you worked hard to achieve something. What was it? What helped you achieve it?

Global reading

Look at the questions about William Kamkwamba. Then read *Making a difference* and make notes on the answers.

1 What was William's life like when he was growing up?
2 Describe what education he has had.
3 What helped him achieve his goal?
4 What are some of his other achievements?

Close reading

> **IDENTIFYING IMPORTANT DETAILS**
>
> Determining your reasons for reading a text will help you decide which information is important. Follow these tips to help you identify important details in a text:
>
> • Before you read, ask yourself, *What do I want to know about this topic? What do I need to know?*
> • When reading an academic text for a class, read any discussion questions first, so you can focus on information you will need to talk about.
> • When taking a test that involves a reading text, read all of the questions and answer choices first.
> • Use your skills for scanning and reading fluently to find information quickly.

Reading skills

READING EXCERPTS Interesting and original topics make up the reading excerpts in *Skillful*.

Read the statements. Then read *Making a difference* again and complete the statements.

1 As a young boy, William was expected to _____
2 Most people in rural Malawi go to bed early because _____
3 In the year 2000, Malawi _____
4 William got the idea to build a windmill from _____
5 At age 14, William _____
6 Today, William's village _____

ACADEMIC KEYWORDS

accept   (v)   /ək'sept/
material   (n)   /mə'tɪriəl/
reality   (n)   /ri'æləti/

Reading skills

Making a difference

[1] Growing up in rural Malawi, Africa, William Kamkwamba learned to accept that life was hard. He lived with his parents and seven sisters in a small clay house without electricity or running water. Like most boys in his village, William was expected to assist his parents on the family farm, as well as keep up with his school work. Each night, like most Malawians, his family went to bed early because the kerosene oil they needed to light the lamps was costly.

[2] A terrible drought in 2000 left many Malawians hungry, and William's family was no exception. In 2003, at the age of 13, William and many other children were forced to drop out of school when their parents could no longer afford the tuition. William had to work even harder to help his family, but he wasn't ready to give up his education. He went to the local library and took out some books to study. One book, called *Using Energy*, sparked William's interest in science and gave him an idea that significantly changed his future.

[3] In the book, William found a picture of a windmill, and a brief description of how it could be used to generate electricity from wind. He knew that there was plenty of wind in his village, and realized that if he could build a windmill like that, he could give his family and the people in his village a much better life.' There was just one problem. The book didn't explain how to build a windmill, and neither did any of the other books in the library.

[4] What happened over the next year demonstrated William's incredible ambition and determination. He began to collect any kinds of materials he thought could be useful—scraps of wood, broken bicycles, old shoes—and started to build a windmill next to his family's house. He endured many challenges and failures. Other people in his village called him crazy and said his idea would never work. Finally, at the age of 14, William completed his first windmill. When they saw electric lights and heard the sound of music on the radio coming from William's house, the village people came running. He had done it. William Kamkwamba had found a way to capture the wind.

[5] Kamkwamba's autobiography, *The Boy Who Harnessed the Wind*, tells the story of how the rest of the world came to know about his achievements. With the help of international supporters, his village now has clean running water, solar powered lighting, and electric power. As a result of his actions, Kamkwamba was invited to study engineering at Dartmouth College, one of the top-ranking universities in the U.S. He also travels the world and gives talks about how he made his dream a reality.

Developing critical thinking

Discuss these questions in a group.

1 Describe your reaction to William's story. How do you think the attitudes of the people in his village changed after his success?
2 What words would you use to describe William's personality? Do you (or does someone you know) share any of the same traits? Which ones?

DEVELOPING CRITICAL THINKING Developing critical thinking is a chance to reflect on issues presented in the text.

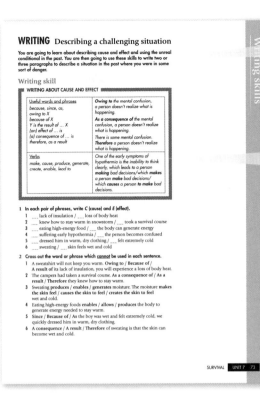

WRITING Describing a challenging situation

You are going to learn about describing cause and effect and using the unreal conditional in the past. You are then going to use these skills to write two or three paragraphs to describe a situation in the past where you were in some sort of danger.

Writing skill

WRITING ABOUT CAUSE AND EFFECT

Useful words and phrases	
because, since, as, owing to X because of X Y is the result of ... X (an) effect of ... is (a) consequence of ... is therefore, as a result	*Owing to* the mental confusion, a person doesn't realize what is happening. *As a consequence of* the mental confusion, a person doesn't realize what is happening. There is some mental confusion. *Therefore* a person doesn't realize what is happening.
Verbs	
make, cause, produce, generate, create, enable, lead to	One of the early symptoms of hypothermia is the inability to think clearly, which leads to a person *making bad decisions/which makes* a person make bad decisions/ *which causes* a person *to make bad* decisions.

1 In each pair of phrases, write C (cause) and E (effect).
1 ___ lack of insulation / ___ loss of body heat
2 ___ knew how to stay warm in snowstorm / ___ took a survival course
3 ___ eating high-energy food / ___ the body can generate energy
4 ___ suffering early hypothermia / ___ the person becomes confused
5 ___ dressed him in warm, dry clothing / ___ felt extremely cold
6 ___ sweating / ___ skin feels wet and cold

2 Cross out the word or phrase which <u>cannot</u> be used in each sentence.
1 A sweatshirt will not keep you warm. **Owing to / Because of / A result of** its lack of insulation, you will experience a loss of body heat.
2 The campers had taken a survival course. **As a consequence of / As a result / Therefore** they knew how to stay warm.
3 Sweating **produces / enables / generates** moisture. The moisture **makes the skin feel / causes the skin to feel / creates the skin to feel** wet and cold.
4 Eating high-energy foods **enables / allows / produces** the body to generate energy needed to stay warm.
5 **Since / Because of / As** the boy was wet and felt extremely cold, we quickly dressed him in warm, dry clothing.
6 **A consequence / A result / Therefore** of sweating is that the skin can become wet and cold.

SURVIVAL UNIT 7 73

SECTION OVERVIEW Giving students the context within which they are going to study the productive skills.

SKILLS BOXES Highlighting writing advice.

FORM AND FUNCTION Notes on form and function match up with Listening & Speaking grammar in the parallel unit.

END OF UNIT TASK Comprehensive end-of-unit task with a noticing exercise for students to identify key features.

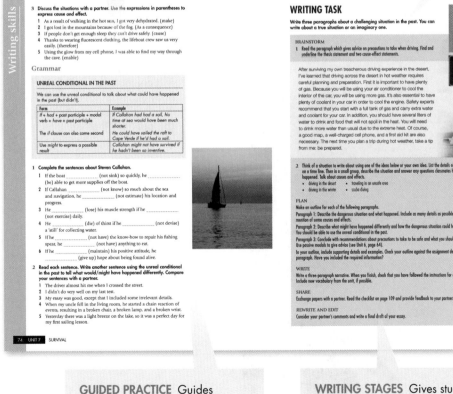

3 Discuss the situations with a partner. Use the expressions in parentheses to express cause and effect.
1 As a result of walking in the hot sun, I got very dehydrated. (make)
2 I got lost in the mountains because of the fog. (As a consequence)
3 If people don't get enough sleep they can't drive safely. (cause)
4 Thanks to wearing fluorescent clothing, the lifeboat crew saw us very easily. (therefore)
5 Using the glow from my cell phone, I was able to find my way through the cave. (enable)

Grammar

UNREAL CONDITIONAL IN THE PAST

We can use the unreal conditional to talk about what could have happened in the past (but didn't).

Form	Example
If + had + past participle + modal verb + have + past participle	If Callahan had had a sail, his time at sea would have been much shorter.
The if clause can also come second	He could have sailed the raft to Cape Verde if he'd had a sail.
Use might to express a possible result	Callahan might not have survived if he hadn't been so inventive.

1 Complete the sentences about Steven Callahan.
1 If the boat _____ (not sink) so quickly, he _____ (be) able to get more supplies off the boat.
2 If Callahan _____ (not know) so much about the sea and navigation, he _____ (not estimate) his location and progress.
3 He _____ (lose) his muscle strength if he _____ (not exercise) daily.
4 He _____ (die) of thirst if he _____ (not devise) a 'still' for collecting water.
5 If he _____ (not have) the know-how to repair his fishing spear, he _____ (not have) anything to eat.
6 If he _____ (maintain) his positive attitude, he _____ (give up) hope about being found alive.

2 Read each sentence. Write another sentence using the unreal conditional in the past to tell what would/might have happened differently. Compare your sentences with a partner.
1 The driver almost hit me when I crossed the street.
2 I didn't do very well on my last test.
3 My essay was good, except that I included some irrelevant details.
4 When my uncle fell in the living room, he started a chain reaction of events, resulting in a broken chair, a broken lamp, and a broken wrist.
5 Yesterday there was a light breeze on the lake, so it was a perfect day for my first sailing lesson.

74 UNIT 7 SURVIVAL

WRITING TASK

Write three paragraphs about a challenging situation in the past. You can write about a true situation or an imaginary one.

Audience:	classmates/peers
Context:	school newspaper
Purpose:	to describe a dangerous situation

BRAINSTORM
1 Read the paragraph which gives advice on precautions to take when driving. Find and underline the thesis statement and two cause-effect statements.

After surviving my own treacherous driving experience in the desert, I've learned that driving across the desert in hot weather requires careful planning and preparation. First it is important to have plenty of gas. Because you will be using your air conditioner to cool the interior of the car, you will be using more gas. It's also essential to have plenty of coolant in your car in order to cool the engine. Safety experts recommend that you start with a full tank of gas and carry extra water and coolant for your car. In addition, you should have several liters of water to drink and food that will not spoil in the heat. You will need to drink more water than usual due to the extreme heat. Of course, a good map, a well-charged cell phone, and a first aid kit are also necessary. The next time you plan a trip during hot weather, take a tip from me: be prepared.

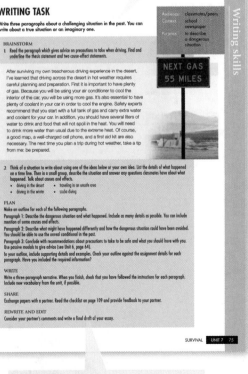

2 Think of a situation to write about using one of the ideas below or your own idea. List the details of what happened on a time line. Then in a small group, describe the situation and answer any questions classmates have about what happened. Talk about causes and effects.
• driving in the desert • traveling in an unsafe area
• driving in the winter • scuba diving

PLAN
Make an outline for each of the following paragraphs.
Paragraph 1: Describe the dangerous situation and what happened. Include as many details as possible. You can include mention of some causes and effects.
Paragraph 2: Describe what might have happened differently and how the dangerous situation could have been avoided. You should be able to use the unreal conditional in the past.
Paragraph 3: Conclude with recommendations about precautions to take to be safe and what you should have with you. Use passive modals to give advice (see Unit 6, page 64).
In your outline, include supporting details and examples. Check your outline against the assignment details for each paragraph. Have you included the required information?

WRITE
Write a three-paragraph narrative. When you finish, check that you have followed the instructions for each paragraph. Include new vocabulary from the unit, if possible.

SHARE
Exchange papers with a partner. Read the checklist on page 109 and provide feedback to your partner.

REWRITE AND EDIT
Consider your partner's comments and write a final draft of your essay.

SURVIVAL UNIT 7 75

GUIDED PRACTICE Guides students through the stages of a writing task.

WRITING STAGES Gives students support through the stages of the writing process.

VISUAL WALKTHROUGH 7

STUDY SKILLS WITH STELLA COTTRELL

Information on study skills features at the end of every unit. Some of these pages showcase a task from Stella Cottrell's bestselling title *The Study Skills Handbook*.

STUDY TIPS Stella offers students useful and memorable tips to improve their studying methods through self-reflection and critiquing.

Using desired outcomes to guide study strategy

by Stella Cottrell

Your reasons for studying and your desired outcomes can guide the way you proceed with your study, as in the following examples.

Outcome A: to learn about the subject

If learning about the subject is the most important outcome for you, then reading around the subject and doing what interests you may be more important than following the curriculum.

Outcome B: to have a good grade

If your main priority is getting a good grade, then it is likely to be important that you 'play the game' and find out exactly what is required.

Outcome C: just to get through

If you have many other demands on your time, or gaps in your education, you may have to limit yourself to covering essentials. What is important is that you know how to find and use information to get you through — you can fill gaps in your knowledge later in life.

Stating your desired outcomes

Outcomes are most motivating when stated in the present:
I am able to achieve a 2.1!

It is also best to state them as positive objectives:
I am able to gain a good job.

(Negatively formed outcomes, such as 'A degree will help me to escape from my current employment', are less effective in providing motivation.)

> **The effect of thinking negatively**
> Having a negative outcome is like going shopping with a list of what you are not going to buy.
> O'Connor and McDermott (1996)

Analyze desired outcomes in detail

The following questions are based on an approach known as Neuro-Linguistic Programming (NLP).

Are your desired outcomes 'well-formed'?
- Are the desired outcomes clear and specific?
- Are they at all limiting?
- Do they help you?
- Are they realistic?
- Are they sufficiently motivating?
- Are the outcomes worth it?
- Are they really desirable?
- How will you know you have achieved the outcomes — what will be different?

What are the implications of having these desired outcomes?
- Will you need to put everything else on hold?
- Will you have to change your study options?
- Who else will be affected?
- Are there other implications?

What are the potential gains?
- Will you feel more in control of your life?
- Will you have more respect for yourself?
- Are there other potential gains?

What are the potential losses?
- Will you see less of family and friends?
- What sacrifices are involved?
- Are there other potential losses?

Visualize yourself in the future, having achieved the outcome
- Where are you as a result of your achievement?
- Are there any good or bad consequences?
- What has changed for you?
- Are you as happy as you thought you would be?

STUDY SKILLS Using the thesaurus

Getting started

Discuss these questions with a partner.
1 What type of dictionary do you use? What information does it include?
2 Do you use a dictionary to help you when you are writing? How does it help you?
3 Have you ever used a thesaurus to find synonyms (or antonyms)? When? For what types of writing?

Scenario

Read the scenario and think about what Kumar is doing right and what he is doing wrong.

Consider it

Look at these tips for using a thesaurus. Which ones do you already follow? Which ones are most useful to you?

1 **Know the benefits** The average thesaurus contains over 100,000 synonyms for words. Using a thesaurus can help you build your vocabulary, avoid repetition in your writing, express your ideas more accurately, and make your descriptions richer and more interesting.
2 **Know when to use it** Use a dictionary when you want to know the meaning of a particular word. Use a thesaurus when you already have a word in mind but feel that it does not express exactly what you want to say, when you want to avoid repeating a word in a passage, or when you are looking for a more (or less) formal/poetic/scientific, etc. word.
3 **Choose the right type** There are two types of thesaurus: those for general use are organized alphabetically, like a dictionary; the other type organizes words by theme or topic (e.g. medicine, music).
4 **Learn the features** In addition to synonyms, a thesaurus may list antonyms or contain topical word lists or other useful features.
5 **Be aware that synonyms aren't exact translations** No two words have exactly the same meaning nor convey the same tone, feeling, or level of formality. When in doubt, use the dictionary to double check meaning to help you make a choice for which word to choose.
6 **Check out electronic and online options** These days, many electronic dictionaries have thesaurus features. Smartphones have downloadable thesaurus apps, and there are many thesaurus websites. Choose the option that works best for you.

> Kumar enjoys writing in English, and he even keeps an English journal, which he uses as a diary and for writing short stories and poems. This semester, he is taking a creative writing course for English majors. Sometimes he finds it hard to express his ideas because he isn't sure of the right vocabulary in English. He sometimes uses the dictionary when he wants to know the English translation for a word in his own language, but he finds it annoying to have to stop his writing often and check a big, bulky book. In these cases, he just uses simple words he already knows in English that have a similar meaning to the word in his first language. Two consistent comments from Kumar's writing teacher are that he should try to use more descriptive language in his writing and he needs to avoid repetition of the same words.

Over to you

Discuss these questions with a partner.
1 Which type of thesaurus would be most convenient and useful for you (e.g. printed book, electronic, online, alphabetical, topical)? Why?
2 What are the potential disadvantages of using a thesaurus?
3 What additional features would you ideally like to have in your thesaurus (e.g. antonyms, word lists, pronunciation information)? Why?

STUDY SKILLS SCENARIOS Using original material, the other end-of-unit study skills task gives students a positive or negative scenario to work through. This provides them with the opportunity for personal performance reflection.

SKILLFUL VERSATILITY Both student and teacher facing, the *Skillful* Digibook can be used for group activities in the classroom, on an interactive whiteboard, or by the student alone for homework and extra practice.

DIGIBOOK TOOLBAR The toolbar that appears on each page allows for easy manipulation of the text. Features such as highlighting and a text tool for commenting allow the teacher to add points as the class goes along, and functions like the zoom and grab tool means the teacher can focus students' attention on the appropriate sections.

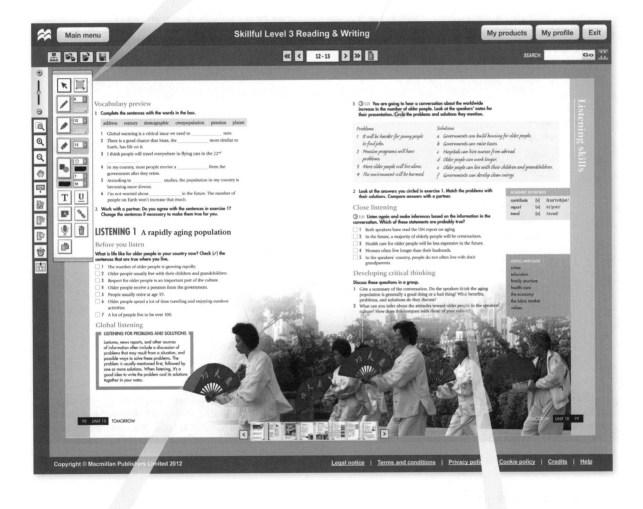

EMBEDDED AUDIO For instant access to the audio for unit exercises, the Digibook has embedded files that you can reach in one click.

PAGE-FAITHFUL Provides a digital replica of the *Skillful* Student's Books while hosting additional, interactive features.

WHAT IS *SKILLFUL* PRACTICE? The *Skillful* practice area is a student-facing environment designed to encourage extra preparation, and provides additional activities for listening, vocabulary, grammar, speaking, and pronunciation as well as support videos for listening and alternative unit assignments.

Main Menu > Skillful practice... >   Skillful - Level 1 Reading and Writing   My products   My profile   Exit

Skillful practice
Use the tree below to find the resources you need

▼ Main Menu
  Digibook
  ▼ Skillful practice
    ▼ Unit 1
      Vocabulary
      Global reading skill
      Close reading skill
      Close reading skill 2
      Vocabulary skill
      Writing skill
      Grammar skill 1
      Grammar skill 2
      Writing task
      Video activity
    ► Unit 2
    ► Unit 3
    ► Unit 4
    ► Unit 5

^ Main Menu   << Digibook   Markbook >>

Copyright © Macmillan Publishers Limited 2013   Credits | Terms and conditions | Privacy Policy | Cookie policy | About us | Help

UNIT AND TASK SELECTION
Handy drop-down menus allow students to jump straight to their practice unit and the exercise they want to concentrate on.

TEACHER RESOURCES The *Skillful* teachers have many more resources at their fingertips.

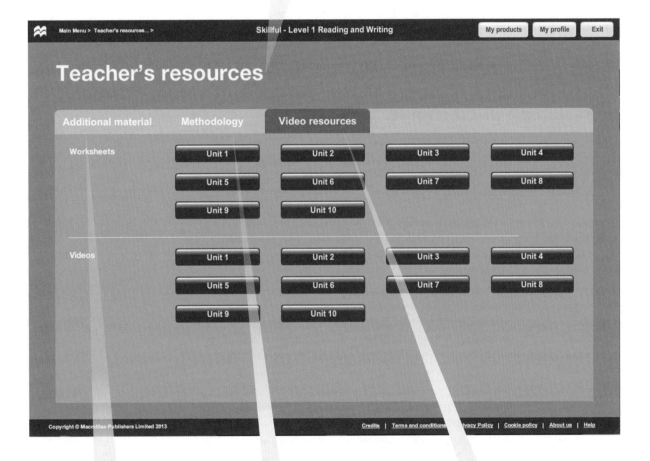

ADDITIONAL MATERIAL Along with the student add-ons there are printable worksheets, test materials, and a markbook component to grade and monitor student progress.

METHODOLOGY For teachers who may need a little extra help to effectively utilize all of the resources *Skillful* has to offer, there are course methodology notes.

VIDEO RESOURCES Teachers have access to the same videos as the students, and to complement these there are printable video worksheets to aid lesson planning.

To the teacher

Academic success requires so much more than memorizing facts. It takes skills. This means that a successful student can both learn and think critically. *Skillful* helps teachers prepare their students for academic work in English by teaching not only language—vocabulary and grammar—but the necessary skills to engage with topics, texts, and discourse with classmates.

Skillful gives students:

- engaging texts on a wide variety of topics, each examined from two different academic disciplines
- skills for learning about a wide variety of topics from different angles and from different academic areas
- skills they need to succeed when reading and listening to these texts
- skills they need to succeed when writing for and speaking to different audiences
- skills for critically examining the issues presented by a speaker or a writer
- study skills for learning and remembering the English language and important information.

Teachers using *Skillful* should:

- Encourage students to ask questions and interact. Learning a language is not passive. Many of the tasks and exercises involve pairwork, groupwork, and whole-class discussion. Working with others helps students solidify their understanding and challenge and expand their ability to think critically.

- Personalize the material. Help students make connections between the texts in their book and their own world—home, community, and country. Bring in outside material from local sources when it's relevant, making sure it fits the unit topics and language.

- Provide a lot of practice. Have students do each exercise several times, with different partners. Review exercises and material from previous units. Use the *Skillful* Digibook to develop the skills presented in the Student's Book. Have students complete the additional activities on a computer outside of class to make even more progress. Assign frequent manageable review tasks for homework.

- Provide many opportunities for review. Remind students of the skills, grammar, and vocabulary they learned in previous units. Have students study a little bit each day, not just before tests.

- Show students how to be independent learners. Point out opportunities to study and practice English outside of class, such as reading for pleasure and using the Internet in English. Have them find and share information about the different unit topics with the class. The *Study skills* section in every unit gives students valuable tips for successfully managing their own learning.

Learning skills, like learning a language, takes time and practice. Students must be patient with themselves as they put in the necessary time and effort. They should set and check goals. Periodic assessments the teacher can print, such as the unit tests, progress tests, and end test on the Digibook let students see their own progress and measure how much they've learned, so they can feel proud of their academic and linguistic development.

The *Skillful* blend by Dorothy E. Zemach

In some academic disciplines, students can begin by acquiring a lot of facts and general knowledge. In a language, however, students need far more than information—they need skills. They need to know how to do things: how to explain, persuade, ask for help, extend an invitation, outline and argue a thesis, distinguish between important and unimportant information, follow digressions, understand implied information, and more.

Skillful recognizes that skills such as these can't be learned by memorizing facts. To acquire these skills, students must notice them as they read or listen; break them down and understand them through clear explanations; and then rehearse and apply those skills in carefully scaffolded activities that lead to freer practice.

The listening and reading texts in each unit introduce students to one subject area explored through two different academic disciplines and two distinct genres. Students learn and practice both global skills, such as recognizing tone and identifying the main idea, and close skills, such as understanding pronoun references and figuring out vocabulary from context, to understand the texts on several levels.

These days, students must interact with both digital and printed text, online and offline, in the classroom and in the workplace. The *Skillful* textbooks are therefore supplemented with the *Skillful* Digibooks. These further develop, explain, and extend the skills work found in the printed textbooks. They provide additional exercises related to the skills, the grammar points, and the vocabulary areas. They can be accessed either via the Digibook or through the *Skillful* practice area. Scores are tracked and recorded and if students work offline, their markbook will be updated the next time they connect to the Internet.

Videos for each unit provide additional subject area content that review the skills and language taught in the unit. The videos can be shown in class to feed in additional content and the accompanying worksheets can be used to structure the lesson.

Unit checklists help students keep track of language in the unit and review for tests.

The Digibooks also help teachers with classroom organization and management by assigning and tracking homework and monitoring student progress using the markbook. A full suite of test materials can be used for placement into the appropriate level and then provide end-of-unit tests and end-of-course tests that can be used as both formative assessments (to evaluate progress) and summative assessments (to mark achievements and assign grades). Tests are provided in both editable and non-editable formats enabling teachers to manipulate the content, as desired. The format of these tests is similar to internationally recognized standardized tests.

Dorothy E. Zemach taught ESL for over 18 years, in Asia, Africa, and the U.S. She holds an MA in TESL and now concentrates on writing and editing ELT materials and conducting teacher training workshops. Her areas of specialty and interest are teaching writing, teaching reading, business English, academic English, and testing.

Teaching study skills by Stella Cottrell

There is a growing awareness that students' performance, even in higher education, can be improved through training in relevant academic skills. Hurley (1994) described study skills as "key skills for all areas of education, including advanced study" and argued that students benefit when these skills are taught explicitly. In other words, it should not be assumed that the skills a student brings from school, or even from the first year of university, are sufficient to carry them through their degree. Skills such as task management, working with others, and critical thinking need to be fine-tuned and extended as students move from one level to another.

Globally, universities and colleges are giving far more attention to preparatory support for prospective students and to developing study skills once a student is on a programme. In some countries, there is a growing emphasis, too, on "employability skills," from soft skills such as communication, creativity, and working collaboratively to new attributes sought by employers, including business acumen, cross-cultural sensitivity, and enterprise. In addition, each institution tends to identify a range of skills and qualities that it wants to see embodied by its graduates.

One of the challenges is articulating what is meant by study skills in this changing environment. This has significance for students when trying to make sense of long lists of skills that they are expected to accumulate during their time in higher education. It also has a bearing on who teaches and supports study skills. In some colleges and universities this falls to study skills specialists; in others, it may be allocated to teaching staff. In each case, different approaches are used to make sense of the learning experience.

From the students' perspective, it helps to organize study skills into a few, relatively easy-to-remember categories. In the latest version of *The Study Skills Handbook*, I suggest using four basic categories:

1 Self   2 Academic   3 People   4 Task

The starting place for students is being able to manage themselves within a new learning environment with confidence and resilience. They need to understand the rationale for, and benefits of, independent study and the kinds of challenges that they will be set. This involves organizing their time, coping with deadlines, and recognizing what it means to take charge of their own learning. It also includes metacognitive skills in reflecting on how they think, learn, and manage themselves for study.

Academic skills consist of such skills as the core research skills (finding, recording, and using information), thinking skills (critical thinking skills, creative problem-solving, and synthesis); understanding academic conventions (the nature and integrity of academic study), and writing skills.

People skills are increasingly important as collaborative study becomes a feature of higher education. These include such skills as giving and receiving criticism, supporting others without cheating, group project work, and playing an active role in group sessions. These can be an especial challenge for international students who may be used to different kinds of learning interactions.

Task management skills within this learning context include such skills as meeting given requirements and using appropriate protocols and project management in order to achieve a given academic task such as writing an essay or report, undertaking research, conducting an experiment, or solving a problem.

An additional value of this framework is that the basic shell can be easily adapted to other contexts, such as employability. The "Self / People / Tasks" model is one that I used, for example, within *Skills for Success: Personal Development and Employability (2010)*.

Stella Cottrell is Director for Lifelong Learning at the University of Leeds, U.K. She is author of the bestselling *The Study Skills Handbook, The Palgrave Student Planner, The Exam Skills Handbook, Critical Thinking Skills, Study Skills Connected,* and *Skills for Success,* all published by Palgrave Macmillan.

Reference
Hurley, J. (1994), *Supporting Learning* (Bristol: The Staff College and Learning Partners).

Teaching academic vocabulary by Pete Sharma

It has been estimated that in an academic text, a quarter of the words are either "academic vocabulary" or "technical vocabulary." What is "academic vocabulary"? The term includes:

- concepts, such as *research*
- actions, such as *classifying* and *defining*
- nouns, such as *sources* and *references*
- collocations, such as *reading list*, and
- reporting, language such as *argue*.

Academic vocabulary is used across all disciplines. This essay will describe a range of activities for teaching academic vocabulary.

Students meet and practice new vocabulary in every kind of lesson, and especially in reading and listening lessons. In a listening lesson, you may pre-teach key vocabulary before students do the listening task. Similarly, in a reading lesson, you can pre-teach specific words to make the text easier to read. Throughout the *Skillful* Students' Book, there are "Vocabulary skill" boxes, and "Academic keyword" boxes which signal important words.

Giving presentations provides opportunities for students to use and practice new vocabulary, and for you to provide feedback on their pronunciation. Similarly, writing essays allows learners to produce the new words they have learnt in context.

During the course, you will not only present and practice vocabulary but also give advice on effective learning strategies. Explore the different ways students can record the new vocabulary they meet on the course. Many students merely jot down a word and write a translation next to it, so it is helpful to present alternatives, such as creating "word trees." Have students work together to create mind-maps on relevant topics, as we remember words when we meet them in concept groups. The *Skillful* Teacher's Book includes several ideas for using a vocabulary notebook. Point out that many words have a standard meaning and an academic meaning. Give examples: references; argument.

Students frequently start their academic course over-using their bilingual dictionary. They benefit from a lesson or lessons exploring the pros and cons of using a monolingual, English–English dictionary. A good way to start a dictionary lesson is to do a quiz to show some useful features in the dictionary. Part of a lesson can be spent introducing learners to electronic dictionaries, which allow students to listen to new words. You can demonstrate a CD-ROM and web-based dictionary using a data projector.

There are several important features of academic vocabulary that you will wish to focus on during the course. It is useful to provide practice on prefixes and suffixes, since noticing patterns in the language can help learners work out the meaning of new words. Also, focus on "collocation" or "word partnerships." Before students read a text, you can select some key collocations, write them on cards, and get students to match them. Students can then scan the text and highlight these collocations before moving to more intensive reading practice. There are several language exercises on prefixes, suffixes, and collocations in *Skillful* and the Teacher's Book also contains sets of photocopiable cards which can be used in many ways, as warmers for example, or for reviewing lexis.

There is no need to develop a new methodology for teaching academic vocabulary. Good practice involves students meeting new words in context, practicing them in speaking and writing, and recycling them in a variety of ways. Working through the units and different levels of *Skillful* will enable students to practice and review academic vocabulary systematically.

Pete Sharma is an associate Lecturer at Oxford Brookes University, U.K. He has written books on technology in language teaching, and is co-author of *Blended Learning* (Macmillan: 2007) and *400 Ideas for Interactive Whiteboards* (Macmillan: 2010).

SPECIALIST ESSAYS 15

Educational culture by Stacey H. Hughes

Most language teachers have an understanding of culture and the differences that can arise in culturally diverse situations. By extension, when it comes to the classroom, it is important to consider the mix of culture that our students bring into the classroom, that teachers bring into it, and the cultural expectations of the institution itself. Each culture has its own expectations of the role of the teacher, the students, the material, and the aim of education. Unmet expectations can lead to frustration on the part of the teacher, and poor learning or lack of achievement and dwindling motivation on the part of the learners. It is therefore important to be acutely aware of behavioral and learning expectations.

What is good learning? What is good teaching?

Every educational setting has an idea of what good education means. Teachers and students tend to assume that they share ideas about how to teach and how to learn, or about what good teaching and learning is. However, concepts of "good student" and "good teacher" vary widely from culture to culture. Consequently, students attending university in a foreign country for the first time often have to go through a difficult adjustment period as they learn to adapt to their new educational culture. There are a number of areas that students will need to adjust to. These include differences in teaching style and methodology, differences in what is expected of students in terms of output and behavior, and differences in the expectation of the university itself.

Teacher / student roles and expectations

So, how do educational expectations vary across cultures? Firstly, teacher and student roles and expectations vary widely. For example, teachers in many East Asian classrooms expect their students to be active listeners, and what it means to be a good student is to listen carefully and reflect on the knowledge the teacher is imparting. In other words, they expect students to master the knowledge and skills that they and the coursebook impart. Similarly in many Middle Eastern cultures, the teacher expects the students to memorize what they present. By contrast, in the West, students are expected to ask questions and think critically. Accepting without question is not necessarily a sign of good learning. As to student expectations, in many countries, students expect the teacher to be the authority figure who knows all the answers, or even a moral leader. This expectation can contrast sharply with a culture such as that of the U.K. where teachers are not necessarily expected to have all the answers.

Classroom organization and methodology

Classroom organization and teaching or methodological style can vary as well. In U.K. university classrooms, for example, the atmosphere tends to be less formal, with teachers using humor, emphasizing student participation and debate, and even encouraging students to disagree with them. Active participation is seen as evidence of learning. Teachers also feel students should reflect on their own work and be able to critique the work of their peers. Desks may be arranged in groups or in a semi-circle to facilitate interaction. These differences can feel quite strange to students who are used to a more formal classroom setting and who would not expect importance to be placed on their personal views. While group assignments may be given in Asian and Middle Eastern cultures as well, the classroom setting may tend to be more lecture-orientated.

In conclusion, it is clear that teachers and students bring educational expectations with them into the classroom and that critical thinking, evaluation, reflection, discussion, and learner autonomy are important elements. However, it may be difficult for teachers to know how to bridge the gap between themselves, the students, and the methodology. What is needed firstly is for teachers to be aware of their own underlying cultural expectations and how these are manifested in their teaching practice. They then need to consider whether this classroom practice incorporates the kinds of skills that will help students reach their educational potential in the twenty-first century. And finally, teachers need to spend class time on learner training. It is important for teachers and students to spend this time discussing teaching and learning expectations and roles. Students will most likely not have an awareness of their own educational expectations or that there are any other cultures of education. Teachers need to give a rationale for the skills necessary for EAP and anticipate such questions as, "Why are we doing this?" Stating aims may not be enough. Teachers need to think of how those aims are perceived at the cultural level and help students acculturate to the expectations and requirements of the educational culture they are in.

Stacey H. Hughes is a lecturer at Oxford Brookes University. Her main interests in ELT are learner engagement, active learning, critical thinking, and intercultural issues.

Teaching reading strategies by Jennifer Bixby

As teachers of reading, our goal is to help students improve their reading skills so that they can successfully read English texts such as online news reports, course assignments, or product reviews at work. By giving students a variety of reading strategies, we help them take steps toward becoming independent readers.

Most of us are strong readers in our first language, and many of our students are, too. Without even thinking about it, we apply strategies, read with fluency, think critically, and synthesize what we read. However, just like our students, when we are faced with a text in a new language, all of those good practices seem to fly out the window. We too want to grab a dictionary to check unknown words; we forget to skim for the main idea or to read fluently to the end. When we abandon our reading strategies, comprehension drops.

One way to help students become better readers is to explicitly teach and practice good reading strategies such as predicting, scanning, and guessing meaning from context in the classroom. Although they may be second nature to us, reading strategies are not habits for many students. Using class time to practice skills encourages students to use them independently and automatically, even outside of the classroom.

Some basic strategies may seem unnecessary and perhaps even a waste of class time. Take, for example, the strategy of previewing a text before reading. Strong readers do this so automatically that they are not even aware of it. Yet previewing leads to increased comprehension, and is a step that shouldn't be skipped. Previewing can be compared to preparing to dive into a lake. You don't just run to the edge and dive in. You survey the scene, look at the water's surface, and think about what might be underneath the water. You wonder how deep it might be, how cold it might be, and how far you might swim. All of this goes through your mind very quickly, but it prepares you to dive in. In the same way, in the classroom, students need to stop and preview the text before they "dive into" the reading. By previewing in class, students develop a valuable habit that research has shown increases comprehension.

Teaching students to self-monitor as they read is another in-class activity that fosters independence in reading. Students can self-monitor by taking notes as they read, summarizing each paragraph, or underlining key concepts or facts. While these seem like easy tasks, students need the opportunity to practice these skills over and over. When students monitor their comprehension as they move through a text, they are interacting with it and becoming active readers. These are essential skills for academic success.

Building fluency also strengthens students' reading. Often students stop for unknown words and therefore do not have the experience of moving forward at a steady rate as they read. To help students increase speed and fluency, give them a short amount of time to read a passage. Have them stop after five minutes and simply mark where they stopped. Then have them read the passage again for five minutes, marking where they stop. By the third reading, students will see that with familiarity, they can increase their reading speed. Just as swimmers practice to increase their speed, so can readers.

Finally, encourage students to read outside of class. Extensive reading builds vocabulary and helps develop an awareness for how ideas are usually phrased, a sort of language muscle-memory. Students can build reading fluency by reading material that is at a slightly lower level of difficulty. Provide students with a good selection of short, level-appropriate texts from which to choose. This will provide the satisfaction of finishing what they read without a great deal of effort, and encourage students to become independent readers.

When we explicitly teach strategies, we help students improve their reading skills and become more autonomous in their reading. Devoting classroom time to the development of these skills has very real benefits, and with time, students will become independent and skillful readers both in and out of class.

Jennifer Bixby holds an M.A. in TESOL from Boston University. She has been an ELT teacher in Colombia, Japan, and the U.S. in a wide variety of programs. An experienced ELT writer, editor, and published author, her main interests are in teaching reading and writing.

UNIT 1 IDENTITY

Reading	Previewing
	Understanding key terms
	Identifying the main idea
Vocabulary	Choosing the right word form
Writing	Paragraph structure
Grammar	Clause joining with subordinators

As this is the first day of class, it is a good idea to spend some time getting to know the students and making sure they get to know a little about each other. Once the ice is broken, students will feel more comfortable discussing the questions in the book with each other. Ask the students to make a 5 x 6 table on a sheet of paper. In the left-hand column, starting in row 2, ask them to write five questions that they might ask someone whom they have never met before. Next, ask them to interview the person sitting next to them, noting the answers in their table. Ask them to stand up and find four other people to interview using the same set of questions. Ask some students to give feedback at the end.

Discussion point

Draw students' attention to the picture on page 7. Ask: *What does it show? How does the boy feel? Why does he have face paint on? How is the picture connected to the topic of identity?* (Many sports fans identify strongly with their team.)

You could initiate a discussion about teams the students support or identify with, the colors of their teams, and if they paint their faces for games or dress in certain colors. Why do they think people identify so strongly with a certain team?

Write the word *identity* on the board and ask students if they know what part of speech it is (noun). Elicit the verb form and note the collocation *to identify with someone / something.* Ask students if they know any other words related to *identity* (*identification, identifiable, identical, identically*). Word forms come up later in the unit, so this is a good introduction to them.

After the group discussion, ask pairs to discuss the three questions in groups. As this is the first lesson, you might need to give some guidance about the importance of speaking in pairs—to give students extra speaking practice and autonomy. Although part of the aim of the *Discussion point* section is to build fluency, some students might feel that it is not worthwhile, unless the teacher is correcting them, so it may be worth spending some time discussing the value of pairwork. For students who really want teacher feedback, you could circulate, listening to various pairs and taking notes on any language issues you hear. These could then be used in a later feedback session. After the students have finished discussing the questions, ask some of the pairs to share their ideas with the rest of the class.

Vocabulary preview

It is a good idea to discourage students from using bilingual dictionaries. You could explain to them that, especially at upper levels, monolingual dictionaries are far more useful because they give more information (word form, multiple definitions, examples of usage, collocations, level of formality, pronunciation guide, etc.). If possible, bring in some monolingual dictionaries for students to use, or ask them to purchase one. Spend some time showing them how they are organized. Alternatively, you could access the Macmillan online dictionary (www.macmillandictionary.com) and show some of its features. The advantage of such an online dictionary is that you can click on the word to hear either the American or the British pronunciation of the word. Students can also access the dictionary on their smartphones.

Ask students to work either in pairs or individually to match the words, allowing the use of monolingual dictionaries. Check answers and drill the pronunciation of the words. Ask students what part of speech each word is (noun, verb, adjective, or adverb).

Now would be a good time to introduce the idea of a vocabulary notebook—this could be collected and monitored periodically. Ask students to write down the words in a vocabulary notebook, noting the part of speech and a sample sentence. They may wish to write a translation of the word as well. There are many ways to organize vocabulary notebooks, but you could have students do them by topic, in this case *identity*. This type of organization is good for studying and recalling words related to a topic.

> **ANSWERS**
> **1** e   **2** a   **3** h   **4** c   **5** b   **6** g   **7** f   **8** d

READING 1 Discuss it online

Word count 396

Background information

Many university courses now include online discussion boards (also known as discussion forums) as part of the course. Professors or students will post a question that students then have to respond to. They are also expected to read each other's postings and may also respond to them, creating a digital discussion. The postings are generally not edited because the purpose is communicability rather than accuracy. Any confusion can be cleared up in the discussion via questions, e.g. *What did you mean by …?*

Discussion boards are a good way to build reflective thinking into the course. Research shows that students who spend time thinking about and reflecting on ideas and issues gain a deeper understanding. In the past, many teachers expected students to write a reflective journal. Discussion boards are similar and may be more appealing to digital-age students. Many students are already familiar with discussion boards and blogs, and feel quite comfortable interacting with course material in this way.

Students who have to complete group projects also find that setting up their own discussion board is a useful way to keep in contact without having to physically meet. For schools that do not have a discussion board platform, it is still possible to set up one via social networking sites, or by using one of the many discussion board and blog platforms available online.

Before you read

Ask students what they think *previewing* means and what it involves. Find out what they do before they read a text in their own language. They may not be aware of the strategies they use, so spend some time brainstorming and discussing their existing reading skills. Afterwards, refer students to the *Previewing* box and ask them to see how many of their ideas are listed. Discuss why asking these kinds of questions is important for reading.

Ask students to use the questions in the box to preview *Discuss it online* on page 9, then discuss their answers in pairs. Have them share their answers with the class.

Global reading

Give students three minutes to read the article and answer the questions. At this point, discourage dictionary use, and encourage students to read quickly for main ideas.

POSSIBLE ANSWERS

1 The instructor wants to have students think about their own identity and relate it to the three aspects of identity before class.
2 He had a bad knee injury and had to quit the soccer team.
3 Ali writes about the values of hard work and competition.
4 During high school, Paul wasn't close with his parents, and his friends influenced him in bad ways.
5 His new friends understand his family background and his values.
6 Ali would probably agree, because even when he had to give up his chosen identity (soccer player), he was still the same person inside.

Close reading

Exam tip

Students cannot use dictionaries in exams, so they must develop the skill of deciphering words from the context. The *Understanding key terms* box gives one strategy for doing this, and students will learn more strategies in later units.

Ask students what they do when they come across a word in a text that they don't know. Hopefully, they will have already developed a few dictionary-free strategies! Ask them to read the *Understanding key terms* box and check they have understood by asking: *Name three ways that key terms are described in academic texts. Where is the definition? Why is it good to write your own definition for a key term?*

Ask students to read *Discuss it online* again and answer the questions. Discourage dictionary use at this stage so that students can focus on finding the definitions of the key terms in the text.

ANSWERS

1 The instructor defines given identity, chosen identity, and core identity.
2 The instructor gives examples for each to help define the term.
3 It is a chosen identity.
4 Answers will vary.

Draw students' attention to the words from the article in the *Academic keywords* box. These are words that frequently occur in academic texts. Ask students to add them to their vocabulary notebooks with a definition or example sentence, and note the part of speech and pronunciation. Make sure the students know how to pronounce the words.

Developing critical thinking

SUPPORTING CRITICAL THINKING

Critical thinking is an important aspect of higher education. The term *critical* in this sense does not mean being negative. It means being thoughtful, being able to evaluate what is read or listened to, and being able to justify arguments and opinions.

Spend a little time introducing the idea of critical thinking. Invite students to think deeply about the critical thinking questions before discussing them in groups. Also, encourage them to give reasons for their opinions and to ask each other questions that will deepen their conversation.

READING 2 Sports fans and identity

Word count 576

Background information

Sports are big business and very much a part of most cultures. Much of the money for teams comes through sponsorship, but a significant amount comes from the sale of products for fans such as team hats, shirts, jackets, and other memorabilia. That's why team owners are interested in fan psychology, or why people support certain teams. By understanding fans' emotional connection to the team, owners can make decisions that will increase and keep their fan base. Owners can also provide more products and increase their revenue if they understand what the fans will buy. Therefore, sociology has a big role to play in modern-day sports.

Before you read

Use the pictures and heading on page 11 to introduce the topic. Remind students of the discussion of sports fans at the beginning of the unit. Ask them to discuss the questions in groups. Draw their attention to the words in the *Useful language* box, making sure they can pronounce them.

Global reading

Exam tip

Many exam questions ask students to identify the main idea in a paragraph or text. It is also an important skill to develop for summarizing. Reading the task or questions before the text (as is required in the *Global reading* activity) is a strategy that works well for exams, because if students know what they are reading for (the purpose), they can read more efficiently, thus saving time.

Ask students what they think *identifying the main idea* means and what it involves, then ask them to read the *Identifying the main idea* box. Find out which method of annotating the main idea students prefer. If they don't have a preferred method, ask them to choose one to use for the *Global reading* exercise.

Ask students to read the instructions and check that they understand what to do before they start. Give them a time limit (e.g. six minutes) to read the statements and then the article without the use of a dictionary. As they read, they should highlight, underline, or make notes in the margin. When the time limit is up, ask them to compare answers, then go over them as a class.

ANSWERS
a 3   **b** 5   **c** 1   **d** 4   **e** X   **f** 2

Use the online Digibook for further practice and reinforcement of vocabulary, reading skills, grammar, and writing skills for each unit. Digibook activities could be set for homework or could be done in class using an interactive whiteboard or projector.

Close reading

1 Encourage students to look at the definitions of the terms in bold in *Sports fans and identity* and provide a definition in their own words. This will practice summarizing skills and will show if students have understood the definition.

ANSWERS
1 Individual identity consists of <u>many things, including our gender, personality, abilities, and social groups.</u>
2 According to social identity theory, <u>we naturally categorize people into groups.</u>
3 Self-esteem means <u>how we feel about ourselves.</u>

2 Ask students to work individually to read the sentences and decide if they are true or false. Encourage them to write full sentences to correct the false statements.

ANSWERS
1 T
2 F (The groups we belong to <u>do</u> influence our self-esteem.)
3 F (Henri Tajfel and John Turner wrote about social identity in sports.)
4 F (Researchers found that fans use different pronouns to talk about their team, depending on if the team won or lost.)
5 T

This is a good place to use the video resource *Shared identity*. It is located in the Video resources section of the Digibook. Alternatively, remind the students about the video resource so they can do this at home.

Developing critical thinking

1 This section refers to the text *Sports fans and identity* only. Students have to form an opinion and give reasons (e.g. examples or evidence) to support it. Supporting opinions with evidence is an important academic skill which will be practiced later in the course, so this exercise is a good introduction. You could ask students to write down their reasons using a graphic organizer such as a word map prior to their discussion. Ask several groups to report back their ideas to the rest of the class. You could use this as an opportunity to list reasons for each statement on the board, thus reinforcing the idea of the importance of backing up opinions with reasons. Alternatively, you could ask groups to summarize their opinions and reasons on a large piece of paper and report back to the whole class.

2 This section refers to the texts *Discuss it online* and *Sports fans and identity*. It is worth spending some time reviewing what *Discuss it online* was about. You could do this as an impromptu, ungraded "quiz" by asking questions about the text (e.g. *What is the main idea of Discuss it online? What is "given identity"?*). Draw students' attention to the words in the *Useful language* box and make sure they can pronounce them. Ask some groups to feed back to the rest of the class.

Ask students to add the words in the *Academic keywords* box to their vocabulary notebooks and review them periodically.

Vocabulary skill

Most students have difficulty in choosing the correct word form, and many do not recognize what form of the word is needed in a sentence. Begin by reviewing the terms *noun*, *verb*, and *adjective*, and brainstorm some examples of each. Ask students to give you a

sentence with some of the words from the brainstorm. You could also write some sentences on the board, and ask students to identify the nouns, verbs, and adjectives. Ask them to read the *Choosing the right word form* box and find two reasons why it is important to recognize word forms. With *confidant* and *confident*, students may not recognize the spelling difference, so be sure to point this out.

1 Check students' pronunciation of tricky words such as *choice* and *choose*, *concern* and *concerned*, and *identity*, *identify*, and *identifiable*. You may wish to check their answers to the chart before asking them to complete the sentences.

2 Ask students to work individually to correct the incorrect word in each question. Check the answers before students discuss the questions with a partner.

WRITING A paragraph about your identity

The writing section is designed to draw the various skills from the unit together in the writing task. It gives a rationale to students for having studied the skills and answers the question, *Why are we doing this?* Ask students to read what they will learn to do in this section and to keep this in mind as they move through the next activities.

Cultural awareness

"Correct" paragraph structure and "good writing" differ according to the language it is written in. It is for this reason that students' writing structure often appears "foreign" or hard to follow. Students who are good writers in their own language may be used to a different kind of structure and will find it difficult to write in the linear way that is the convention of paragraphs in English. Students from some cultures may even see the linear structure as overly simplistic and may resist learning to write in such a naïve or bare bones fashion! Good Chinese paragraphs are circular rather than linear—the topic is never really stated, but is talked around. French and Spanish writing is based on frequent digression from the main topic. Arabic writing uses a lot of parallel structures.

Writing skill

Introduce the topic by brainstorming elements of a good paragraph in English. This will give you an indication of what the students already know about paragraph structure. Ask students to read the *Paragraph structure* box to find out how many of the brainstormed ideas are included.

1   This exercise is designed to guide students to understand the concepts around paragraph structure. If possible, after allowing some time for students to search *Discuss it online*, display the text using the page-faithful part of the Digibook to help point out the text organization.

ANSWERS

1

   a Social psychologists suggest that we have three basic types of identity.

   b three

   c listing organization

   d No, it doesn't.

2

   a When I started high school, I thought that I knew exactly who I was and where I was headed.

   b time order organization

   c Yes, it does.

2   This exercise can be done in pairs or groups on overhead transparencies or large sheets of paper. For those students struggling to list supporting evidence, highlight the main idea of each sentence: 1 = three types of student; 2 = three characteristics of a friend; 3 = three unique abilities. If time allows, you could practice time order organization: provide three topic sentences (e.g. *Three events in my past led me to form my current identity.*) and ask students to list points to support it, including dates

(e.g. *2007, May of last year,* etc.) or expressions of time (*sometime after that, when I was 12,* etc.).

Grammar

There are several problems associated with writing using subordination. Firstly, many students end up writing sentence fragments. A sentence fragment is a subordinate clause used as a sentence, but without being joined to the independent clause. Frequent errors occur with *Because*, e.g. *Because she was clever.* This type of error may occur because students fail to recognize the difference between a dependent and an independent clause. The second common error is known as a comma splice. It occurs when two independent clauses are joined by a comma, but without a conjunction, e.g. *Carmen is outgoing, Latifa is reserved.* The third common error is overuse of the comma. It should go after the dependent clause, not after the independent clause, e.g. *Because she was clever, she got high grades.* ✓ *She got high grades, because she was clever.* ✗ A fourth error occurs when students do not fully understand the meaning of the subordinating word or phrase (cause and effect, contrast, time, etc.). A final error that is characteristic of some language backgrounds is the overuse of dependent clauses in one long, run-on sentence with no periods. This group of students will need to learn to identify the clause types so that they know where to end the sentence.

Introduce the topic by writing two simple sentences on the board: *I started high school. I was very shy.* Firstly, ask students to identify the subject and verb in each sentence. Be sure that they understand why each of them are sentences (each contains a subject and verb and is a complete thought). Introduce the idea of an *independent clause.* Next, ask students to tell you what is wrong with writing two short sentences like that. Brainstorm some ways to combine the sentences. Hopefully, they will come up with a combination that includes an independent and dependent clause, but if not, write up the one in the *Grammar* box: *When I started high school, I was very shy.*

Identify the subjects and verbs, and ask students which part of the sentence can stand alone and why the other part can't. Introduce the idea of *dependent clause* and *subordinating conjunction,* then refer students to the first part of the *Grammar* box.

You may want to categorize the subordinating conjunctions on the board:

Cause and effect: *because, since, if*

Contrast: *although, even though, where*

Time: *when, after, before, until, as soon as*

Make sure students understand the concepts before moving on to the second part of the *Grammar* box, which highlights common errors. Ask students why each one is an error to check they have understood.

1 This exercise ensures students understand the meaning of the subordinating conjunctions within sentences to make logical sense. Point out they must delete the one conjunction that cannot be used in the sentence. When the students have finished, check the answers with the class.

ANSWERS
1 before
2 Before
3 Whenever
4 although
5 if
6 Even though

---

2 This exercise helps students identify sentence fragments and comma splices. Have the students work individually, then check their answers with a partner.

ANSWERS
1 ✗ I didn't understand the theory in physics class.
2 ✗ Although / Even though / After / Because / Since I had many struggles during my first semester, the second semester seemed much easier.
3 ✗ He didn't have much self-confidence because / since he had failed the course twice already.
4 ✓
5 ✗ She was extremely beautiful.
6 ✗ If / When their favorite coach is fired, the fans will be very upset.

WRITING TASK

The writing tasks in *Skillful* follow a process approach, and so are staged to include brainstorming, planning, writing, sharing, rewriting, and editing. Too often students think that writing is just about writing, and they fail to recognize that writing is a process. Many students see the planning stages as a waste of time, and often fail to see the point in editing and rewriting. Students may also feel uncomfortable sharing work with other students or they may not see the point in having another student comment on their work, seeing that as "the teacher's job."

It is worth spending some time discussing the importance of the various stages in the process of writing. Although paragraph models are provided in the units at times (primarily for weaker students), copying models will not build independent writers in the long run.

It is important at the beginning of learning the process approach that the stages are done in class so that the teacher can guide the students through the process, and so that students understand the importance of the process of writing.

The writing tasks also include the audience, context, and purpose of the writing task. This is included partly to add authenticity to the task, but more importantly, these are the things that all writers have to keep in mind when writing. These elements enable writers to pitch their work correctly: at the correct level, with the most effective language for the purpose, with the right degree of formality, with the most effective tone, etc. A personal reflection written to a friend might include slang or text language, for example, or a letter asking a parent for money would use different types of language and discourse than a letter home reporting news.

Ask students to read the writing task and keep it in mind as they go through the next activities. Draw their attention to the box that details the audience, context, and purpose of the writing task. Ask them why it is important to know these things before writing.

Brainstorm

1 Refer the students to the model paragraph. Read the instructions and remind them that they should not complete the model at this point.

ANSWERS
Topic sentence: There are three different aspects that define my identity: my _____ identity, _____ identity, and _____ identity.
Concluding sentence: Of the three aspects of identity, for me my _____ identity is the most important right now.
Subordinating coordinator: I enjoy these groups because …

---

2 Brainstorming is a good way to generate lots of ideas. During a brainstorm, all ideas should be written down—the editing of ideas comes later. You could do this part as a group, or put students into groups or pairs to brainstorm, and then feed back to the whole group.

Plan and write

Spend some time discussing the importance of planning. Find out how many students plan. Emphasize that planning is a time-saving strategy, especially on exams! It also helps to ensure that their writing is well-organized. It is evident to readers when writers have not planned their work! Ask them to follow the steps in the *Plan* section, writing down their answers to the questions. After they have finished, ask them to compare ideas with a partner.

Although many teachers assign writing tasks for homework, it is worth asking students to do writing in class. By observing students writing, teachers can identify any problems students have, how quickly they write, how much they have to use a dictionary, etc.

It is also good exam practice for when students have to write under timed conditions. Finally, it ensures that the students actually do the work themselves!

The model is provided to support weaker students who could use the model and just fill in the spaces with their own ideas if needed. Stronger students can refer to the model, but use their own words.

Share, rewrite, and edit

There are many reasons to get peer feedback on writing, though it may take some time to convince students of its value. The Peer review checklist on page 109 of the Student's Book is designed to guide students in their review of each other's work. Point out that not all the items on the checklist may be relevant to this piece of writing. Tell students they can write on each other's papers. Emphasize that peer review will help them become more independent from the teacher, and that you will only view and mark their second draft. Insisting on this process will indicate to students how important the process is.

Encourage students to consider the comments on their work carefully before rewriting. They may disagree with the comments, but need to think whether they have value or not. This rewriting stage could be done at home. Ask students to turn in the plans and first draft along with their final draft. Use the photocopiable unit assignment checklist on page 88 to assess the students' paragraphs.

STUDY SKILLS Am I a smart reader?

Some of the vocabulary in this section may be new. To introduce the vocabulary, you could write the following words on the board and ask students to tell you where they might find these things, or you could ask them to use their dictionaries to find the meanings: *reading list, source, index, browse, contents page, subheadings, chapter, margins, photocopy, poster, assumptions, logic, validity.*

Ask students to read the title and headings of the *Study skills* section for 30 seconds. Then, ask them to close their books and try to recall as much information as they can. Ask them what the main purpose of the information is and what they think they have to do with it.

Ask students to read the page and check the things that they already do when they read. Spend some time going through some of the ideas and pointing out how they make someone a "smart reader."

For any unchecked ideas, ask students to focus on developing those skills during the course.

EXTENSION ACTIVITY

You may want to revisit this section mid-way through the course, and then again at the end so students can re-evaluate themselves.

Extra research task

Ask students to research and contribute to a blog on sports or another area they are interested in (gardening, knitting, horse racing, etc.). Be sure to warn them about giving out any personal details on a blog. Many bloggers adopt a pseudonym. As an alternative, ask students to research the types of blogs on the Internet today, what they think about sharing information in this way, and whether or not they would ever start up or join a blog.

Reading	Scanning
	Recognizing cause and effect
Vocabulary	Prefix *over-*
Writing	Transitions: introducing opposing ideas
Grammar	Non-defining relative clauses

Discussion point

Lead into the topic by introducing the word *design*. Ask: *What do we mean by design? What kinds of things are designed? Who designs things?* Brainstorm some ideas, then ask students to work in pairs to discuss the questions. During feedback, find out if anyone knows what building is shown in the picture on page 17 (Beijing National Stadium, also known as the Bird's Nest).

It's a good idea to inform students of the skills coming up so that they can have an idea of what they will be learning and connect activities to a purpose. Draw students' attention to the box at the beginning of the unit. After finishing the unit, revisit the box, and ask students to evaluate how well they think they learned the skills and concepts listed.

Ask students to discuss the three questions with a partner. When they have finished, have several pairs share their ideas with the whole class.

The focus of the unit is on design, so before you start, you may wish to get students interested in the theme by using the video resource *The counterfeit wars*. It is located in the Video resources section of the Digibook. Alternatively, remind the students about the video resource so they can do this at home.

Vocabulary preview

Tell students to read the passage first without completing it. Ask them to say what part of speech they think goes in each blank (noun, adjective, verb or adverb). If possible, project the activity onto the board from the Digibook and look at the clues that tell us what part of speech might go into the blank. After students say what part of speech they think each blank needs, ask them to complete the exercise. Allow them to compare answers afterwards. You could also go over the answers by having a student read the text aloud, swapping students after each sentence or two. This will allow some students to practice pronunciation. Afterwards, invite students to add the words to their vocabulary notebooks.

ANSWERS

1	iconic	6	opponents
2	feat	7	landmarks
3	devise	8	priority
4	dilemma	9	Construction
5	eyesore		

EXTENSION ACTIVITY

Revisit the *Vocabulary preview* section in the following class. Write all the words on the board and put the students into pairs. Student A has the book open, Student B has the book closed. Ask Student A to read the text, pausing at each blank. Student B supplies the word. Halfway through, ask them to swap places so that Student B has a chance to supply words. Model the activity first with the first sentence of the passage so that everyone knows what to do.

READING 1 The Metropol Parasol
Word count 495

Background information

European countries such as Spain take interest and pride in their cultural legacy, which is why care is taken to preserve historical buildings. It is recognized that this cultural legacy is not only an expression of ongoing tradition and innovation, but also a source of cohesion in the EU. Added to this is the large economic element—cultural heritage sites draw tourism, which brings in money and creates jobs.

Seville has a very long and diverse history. The Romans were in what is now Seville for around 700 years, beginning around 200 BCE, so is it not surprising that their influence on the culture was significant. At least two Roman Emperors were born in Seville. The city became Muslim around 700 CE, and evidence of this period is still seen in the Moorish architecture today. Seville became Christian in the mid-1200s, and again, some of the architecture reflects that influence.

It is quite common to uncover ancient ruins in old cities such as Seville due to the diverse and long history of the area. Today, Seville is a mixture of old and modern.

Before you read

Ask students to look at the picture on page 18 and discuss the building. Ask: *What kind of building is it? Where do you think it is? What do you think its function is? How would you describe it?*

Have students work in pairs to discuss the question. Ask students to give reasons for what they would build and say who it would be for. Invite students to share their ideas with the rest of the class. You could take a vote on whose idea is the best.

Global reading

1   Give the students two minutes to quickly skim read the article to find out what the Metropol Parasol is. Don't allow dictionaries at this stage. At the end of the time limit, ask them to close their books and discuss their answer with a partner. Have them feed back to the rest of the class.

> **ANSWERS**
> The Metropol Parasol is a public community center in Seville, Spain. It includes shops, restaurants, and cafés, and a museum that exhibits Roman ruins.

Afterwards, point out that this kind of quick reading is called *skim reading*. Students need to understand why skim reading is important. Among other things, reading quickly to get a general idea of what the topic is about will help students become more efficient at deciding what texts are relevant when they do research. In that way, they will be able to judge whether the text is worth spending time reading, or if the content is not really relevant to their topic.

Ask students if they know or can guess what scanning a text involves. They may know the term *scanning* from computing (scanning something onto the computer) or from shopping (scanning the barcode). Ask students to read the *Scanning* box to find out what scanning means in this context.

> **Exam tip**
>
> Most reading exams ask students to find information in a text. Scanning is an important skill to develop so that the information can be found quickly without having to spend time reading information in the text that is not relevant to the exam question. Students should be taught to read the questions first so that they can scan to find the information.

Ask students questions to make sure they understood the information. Ask: *Is scanning quick reading or careful reading? What five things should you look out for when scanning a text? Why is it important to know the questions beforehand? Should you stop and look up words when scanning? What is the difference between skimming and scanning?*

2   Ask students to work with a partner to read the questions and think about the *kinds* of information they will need to find for each one. You may feel it's a good idea to check answers here before proceeding to exercise 3.

> **ANSWERS**
> 1 name of a place (scan for capital letters)
> 2 name of a person (scan for capital letters)
> 3 dates and numbers (scan for numbers)
> 4 numbers (scan for numbers)
> 5 signal words and phrases (scan for *upper level*)

3   Now ask students to scan *The Metropol Parasol* and write short answers to the questions in exercise 2. Set a time limit of around five minutes for this.

> **ANSWERS**
> 1 in Seville, Spain
> 2 German architect, Jürgen Mayer H.
> 3 seven years
> 4 90 million euros
> 5 a panorama deck

Close reading

Some students may feel that they have not fully understood the text based on such a quick reading and without dictionaries! However, point out to them that if they have answered the questions, they have understood a lot. Encourage them to understand that it is not important to understand <u>everything</u> in most texts they read. Ask students to read the sentences and decide if they are true or false. Remind them to correct the false sentences.

> **ANSWERS**
> 1 F (The construction site was originally planned as a parking garage.)
> 2 T
> 3 T
> 4 T
> 5 T

Ask students to find the words in the *Academic keywords* box in the text (they may be in a different form) and highlight the sentences they are in. Ask them to think of other things that you can *preserve* and *convert* (using a word map). Ask them to think of things that are *unique* or of synonyms of *unique*. Finally, ask students to add the words to their vocabulary notebooks.

Developing critical thinking

It is not always necessary that all groups discuss both critical thinking questions. You could divide the class into groups of As and Bs, with Group As answering question 1 and Group Bs answering question 2. You could then ask a Group A and a Group B to work together to share what they discussed. This would be good practice in oral summarizing. To maximize student talking time, ask individuals from Groups A and B to work in pairs and share the discussion the group had.

For question 1, you could ask groups to make two lists—one list summarizing the opinions about the Metropol Parasol, and another listing the advantages and disadvantages of the design. The first list will be useful in the second *Developing critical thinking* section, when students have to discuss the opinions listed in both reading texts.

READING 2 Designing solutions

Word count 675

Background information

Venice is another European city that began as a Roman city. The city we know today was built on 118 small islands in a marshy lagoon around the fifth century CE. Originally, the location was chosen as a temporary refuge from attacks by barbarians, but eventually it grew into a city with great maritime power. As the buildings and pavements took over the sandy islands in the lagoons, the sea surrounding the islands became the canals that we see today. Dozens of footbridges span the canals and connect the city together.

The Nile is one of the longest rivers (if not the longest) in the world. It flows north from North East Africa through ten countries, ending at the Mediterranean Sea in Egypt. At its northern end, the Nile passes through a landscape that is almost all desert. For centuries, the civilizations that have lived along the Nile have depended on the water and especially the yearly floods which have enriched the soil of the floodplain so that crops could be grown. Because the Nile is shared by so many different countries, projects such as the NBI (Nile Basin Initiative) have been set up to ensure that the water is managed adequately for all the countries that rely on it. However, these initiatives have not been very successful, and conflicts over the Nile's water have not been resolved.

Before you read

Use the title *Designing solutions* as a lead-in to the topic. Say: *What do you think the topic means? Solutions to what? If you have a solution, there must be a …?* Divide students into groups and assign each group one of the three areas listed. Ask them to brainstorm the challenges or problems in their area and solutions that have been designed to overcome those challenges. Refer them to the ideas in the *Think about* box. Allow students to use dictionaries to look up the names of specific problems or solutions they don't know in English. You may have to prompt students with some ideas, e.g.

Agriculture / Farming: water shortages → irrigation systems; pests → insecticides; lack of space → vertical planting; steep slopes → terracing

Housing: weather → houses traditionally built for the weather, e.g. steep roofs where there is a lot of snow / flat roofs where there is little rain; high ceilings in hot countries / air conditioning today; space → build up instead of out; energy efficiency → double glazing

Transportation: geographical challenges → bridges over water; banking of roads around curves; curved roads on mountains; weather → drains in roads to avoid flooding.

Ask groups to share ideas with the rest of the class.

Global reading

1 Remind students of the skill of scanning from *The Metropol Parasol*. Ask them to scan quickly for the information and complete the chart.

ANSWERS

Name of project	Location	Year started	Reasons for project
1 New Valley Project	Western Desert, Egypt	1997	to turn area of desert into livable farmland, help solve overcrowding problems
2 Venice Tide Barrier Project	Venice, Italy	2003	to help stop frequent flooding in the city, protect historical landmarks

Lead into the idea of cause and effect by giving some simple examples of visible effects, and asking for the cause, e.g. *I wear glasses—why?* Write up on the board: *cause—I have bad eyes; effect—I wear glasses.* Elicit some other examples. Ask students to make a sentence with one of the examples, e.g. *I wear glasses because I have bad eyes.* Ask them to read the *Recognizing cause and effect* box to find other ways to talk about cause and effect.

Students often get confused about which is the cause and which is the effect, so it is worth spending some time making this clear before moving on. A good graphic organizer to use to show cause and effect is the fishbone diagram; search online using the keywords *fishbone diagram* for examples.

EXTENSION ACTIVITY

Ask students to scan the article, and underline phrases for describing cause and effect relationships. As a follow-up review in the following lesson, give each pair of students a set of cards with the words and phrases from the *Recognizing cause and effect box* (one word or phrase per card), and ask them to put them into two categories: cause → effect; effect → cause.

Design

2 Ask students to read *Designing solutions* again and complete exercise 2.

> **ANSWERS**
> 1 d 2 c 3 f 4 b 5 a 6 e

EXTENSION ACTIVITY

In order to practice using cause and effect language, after matching the causes and effects in exercise 2, ask the students to write sentences using the cause and effect words and phrases. Encourage them to use different expressions. This could be done in pairs and written on overhead transparencies to project, or on big sheets of paper. Sentences will vary. Make sure the sentences make logical sense. Exercises in the Digibook give additional practice of cause and effect language.

Close reading

This activity practices scanning. You may want to do it before *Global reading* exercise 2. As with the first scanning exercise, encourage the students to think of the types of information required before scanning for the answers.

> **ANSWERS**
> 1 population growth, climate change, and aging urban infrastructures
> 2 $436 million
> 3 1.2 million cubic meters per hour
> 4 25%
> 5 as much as 23 centimeters
> 6 28 meters high, 20 meters wide

Ask students to find and highlight the words in the *Academic keywords* box in the text. For a quick filler, ask pairs of students to make a sentence which includes all three words. Ask them to add the words to their vocabulary notebooks.

Developing critical thinking

1 Students can be asked to discuss one or both questions. Encourage them to give reasons for their opinions. To ensure that all students in the group contribute to the conversation, have them keep a tally of the number of times they speak. Compare tallies at the end. Those students with too many marks will need to learn to invite others into the conversation by asking them for their views or by allowing them to speak. Those with too few tallies will need to learn strategies for interrupting or contributing.

EXTENSION ACTIVITY

As a follow-up, you could stage a short debate about one of the projects. Divide the class into two teams—one for the project; the other against. Ask each team to think of reasons to support their stance, then open the debate. For very large classes, several debates can be going on at the same time.

2 This question refers to both *The Metropol Parasol* and *Designing solutions*, so you may need to refresh students' memories about what *The Metropol Parasol* was about. The *Useful language* box contains phrases that are commonly used to report or summarize in academic contexts. Encourage students to use at least one in their discussions. Refer them to the *Think about* box as well if they are having problems generating ideas. Ask the students to work in groups to discuss the questions. When they have finished, have them share their ideas with the whole class.

Vocabulary skill

To lead in, ask students to look at the picture on page 22 and say what the problem is. Elicit or introduce *overflow*. Ask students if they know any other compound words that begin with *over* and what they think *over* might mean. Ask them to read the *Prefix over-* box to check if they are right. Students sometimes try to add *over* to every word to make it mean *too much*, so advise them to check a dictionary if they are not sure. For more examples, type *over* into the *Macmillan Dictionary* online (www.macmillandictionary.com).

For this exercise, students need to add *over* to the words in the box and figure out the best place to put them in the paragraph. Afterwards, they could make a special page for the words in their vocabulary notebooks.

> **ANSWERS**
> 1 overflows   5 overestimated
> 2 overconfident 6 overcrowding
> 3 overslept   7 overdone
> 4 overreacted   8 overeat

EXTENSION ACTIVITY

1 To practice the words in a subsequent lesson, give each pair of students a set of cards face down with the words from the exercise (and any that were brought up in class). Student A takes a card and tries to describe it, and Student B tries to guess the word. Swap after one minute.

2 Students might also like to explore the prefix *under-*. Interestingly, just because you can combine *over* with a word doesn't mean that you can necessarily combine *under* with that word.

WRITING The pros and cons of a design

Be sure to ask students to read what they will learn to do in this section so that they know what is coming up.

To introduce the topic, ask students to look at the picture of the bridge, and brainstorm a list of the pros and cons of its design. Write these on the board. You may have to define *pros and cons* as *positive things and negative things about the design*. You may want to ask students how important they think it is that structures are aesthetically pleasing or if other factors are equally important.

Writing skill

Although all the key words and expressions in this section express opposing ideas, they follow different grammatical patterns.

Although, even though, whereas, and *while* introduce a dependent clause, and are followed by a subject and a verb, e.g. *Although the bridge is attractive, it looks expensive to maintain.*

This is the pattern that students learned about in the *Grammar* section of unit 1 with subordinating conjunctions—including the rule for punctuation. Note that sometimes the ideas are reversible, e.g. *Although it looks expensive to maintain, the bridge is attractive.*

But not always, e.g. *Although the weather was gloomy, we went fishing.* ✓ *Although we went fishing, the weather was gloomy.* ✗

The words *despite* and *in spite of* are not followed by a dependent clause. They are followed by a noun or noun clause and are interchangeable: *Despite / In spite of the attractiveness of the bridge, it looks expensive to maintain.*

Both can introduce a *that* clause, e.g. *In spite of the fact that / Despite the fact that the bridge is attractive, it is expensive to maintain.*

The expression *in contrast to* follows the same grammatical pattern as *despite* and *in spite of*, e.g.

In contrast to the modern style of the bridge, the rest of the city was old.

The second set of expressions are transitions instead of conjunctions, so they must come at the beginning of the second sentence. *However* and *on the other hand* are the most frequently used.

Use some of the ideas generated by the discussion as springboards to the introduction of transitions introducing opposing ideas. For example: *So, you said that the bridge is attractive, but it looks expensive to maintain. We could combine these ideas and say: Although the bridge is attractive, it looks expensive to maintain.*

Ask students to read the *Transitions: introducing opposing ideas* box, and use the sentences and ideas

you wrote on the board to introduce the grammatical difference in the use of each contrasting word or expression. Encourage students to play with different variations of the sentence to check if they are correct or not. Ask them to complete the sentences, and check that they have got the contrast word or expression linked to the right part of the sentence. The Digibook has extra practice deciding which word to use.

ANSWERS
1 The bridge is modern and attractive. However, there are many safety concerns.
2 Although the city needed a new hotel, the building is ugly and won't help attract tourists.
3 Whereas many people like modern, futuristic design, I prefer traditional architecture.
4 The Sky Mall isn't conveniently located. On the other hand, it has amazing views from the rooftop garden.
5 The parking lot may help local businesses. Nevertheless, it will destroy a natural wildlife habitat.

Grammar

Students often don't realize that in non-defining relative clauses the relative pronoun has to follow the noun or noun phrase it refers to, resulting in sentences with misplaced pronouns, e.g.

The Pumping Station cost $436 million to build which was completed in 2005. ✗

It is worth pointing out that the relative pronoun must immediately follow the noun or noun phrase it refers to. It is also important to emphasize that non-defining relative clauses give extra information—almost like an aside. In non-defining relative clauses, *who* and *which* cannot be substituted with *that*, although it could be argued that this rule may be changing with modern English.

Lead in to the grammar section by writing up the sentences from the *Grammar* box on the board, replacing the relative pronoun with a space. Ask students what word they think goes in the space. Ask them to read the *Grammar* box to see if they were right. Check students have understood all the information. Ask: *Do we use "who" with people or things? When do we use "which"? How many commas are in each sentence? Why? Does the non-defining clause add extra information or essential information? What's the difference?*

1 Ask students to complete the sentences and compare answers in pairs. You could encourage students to point out errors in their partner's work if they see any, then check as a group.

2 You could set this exercise for homework and ask students to turn it in to be checked. If you do it in class, invite several students to give their ideas for each sentence, making sure they have used a correct relative clause.

WRITING TASK

Brainstorm

1 Ask students to read the writing task, and draw their attention to the box that details the audience, purpose, and context of the writing task. Check that the students understand the topic, then ask them to read the model text and do the task.

ANSWERS
Transitions:
<u>While</u> the new complex offers lots of state-of-the-art equipment inside, the exterior appears too traditional and rather uninteresting, in my opinion.
<u>However</u>, there are no facilities for sports such as soccer or baseball, which are best played outdoors.
<u>Despite</u> these minor design issues, the Shankman Sports Complex is certain to be a busy place year round.
Non-defining relative clauses:
The new Shankman Sports Complex, <u>which was completed in March 2012</u>, is a brand new sports facility.
The entrance includes some welcoming decorative features, such as a fountain and a statue of the founder, Tom Shankman, <u>who was a minor-league baseball player</u>.
However, there are no facilities for sports such as soccer or baseball, <u>which are best played outdoors</u>.

2 You could ask students to research the topic and print out a picture of it to include with their assignment. Discourage them from copying too much information from the website: limit it to size, location, and purpose.

Plan and write

Make sure students write out their plan. Encourage use of color for those who are visual. They should aim to spend about ten minutes planning.

This time, students have to write two paragraphs of roughly equal length. Tell them to aim for paragraphs of between 75–100 words each. To make a quick approximation of the word count, count every word in one line, then multiply by the number of lines. Students will eventually learn what 75–100 words looks like in their handwriting in terms of page space. For some, it may be an entire page; for others, it will be half a page.

Remind students that they need to include a topic sentence and concluding sentence for each paragraph. Point out to students before they write the following options for setting out their paragraph: they can either indent the first line of the paragraph and not leave an extra line space at the end, or they can choose not to indent the first line, but leave an extra space after the first paragraph to delineate it from the second. It doesn't matter which option they choose; the main thing is that the paragraphs are clearly delineated.

Share, rewrite, and edit

Ask students to read each other's paragraphs and provide feedback. Encourage students to use the Peer review checklist on page 109 of the Student's Book when they are evaluating their partner's paragraph, but also to think about the points listed in the book.

Ask students to rewrite and edit their paragraphs. Encourage them to take into consideration their partner's feedback when rewriting. Ask them to write on a clean piece of paper that is of a standard size if you don't wish to receive papers of various sizes torn out of spiral-bound notebooks. It is easier to comment on papers that are double-spaced. Alternatively, you could ask them to type their papers and give you a printout. Ask them to turn in their plans and first draft also, as this emphasizes their importance, and can give you an indication of the effectiveness of the students' planning and editing. If the first draft was done in class, it can also ensure that it was actually the student who wrote the paper and not someone else!

Use the photocopiable unit assignment checklist on page 89 to assess the students' paragraphs. The checklists at the back of the Teacher's Book are designed so that the language and skills in the unit that the students should have learned are the focus areas for grading. This approach helps motivate students because it breaks down language learning into manageable chunks. Therefore, it gives students a reachable goal to achieve in order to get a good mark.

Use the photocopiable unit assignment checklist on page 89 to assess the students' paragraphs.

EXTENSION ACTIVITY

At the end of each unit or every two units, it is a good idea to do a review of the vocabulary. This could be done as a team competition, which is a motivating way to review. Divide the class into teams. Ask each team to give themselves a name and to write the name on the top of a piece of paper. With books closed, call out a vocabulary word from the unit(s). Decide what you want the groups to do: write a definition; write a sentence; write the word form, etc. Give the teams one minute to come up with an answer, then move on. After 5–10 words, ask the teams to swap papers and go over the answers. The team with the most correct answers wins.

STUDY SKILLS Editing and proofreading strategies

Getting started

A good time to broach the subject of editing and proofreading strategies might be when handing back papers or when assigning a writing task. Write the words *editing and proofreading* on the board, and ask students to brainstorm words associated with them (e.g. *correcting, rewriting, deleting words, adding words, writing more neatly*, etc.).

Put students into pairs and ask them to discuss the questions, then share their ideas with the rest of the class.

Scenario

Ask students to read the scenario, and make a list of what they think Ramon did right and what they think he did wrong. Next, initiate a discussion to find out what students thought.

POSSIBLE ANSWERS

While Ramon was doing the right thing in re-reading his work and checking for errors before handing it in, he needed a better system to help him do a more thorough check. It can be especially difficult to see one's own errors in writing. Becoming familiar with common mistakes, using an editing checklist, and asking a peer to review are helpful habits.

Consider it

The tips are good practice ideas about editing and proofreading. Ask students to read and discuss them with a partner, following the instructions in the book. Find out if anyone has any ideas to add. You may wish to discuss the use of computer editing tools, such as the spelling and grammar checker in word processing programs. Emphasize that, although such tools are useful, they are not always correct and don't find every error. Students still have to use their own editing skills.

Over to you

These questions are a final reflection on editing and proofreading. They would be good questions to answer in a follow-up discussion forum. For question 3, it could be a good opportunity to reinforce the advantages of peer review. Sometimes we are so close to what we write that we can't see our mistakes, but a fresh set of eyes can help. Also, at university, the professor would not normally be expected to look at a first draft of an assignment, and will expect the assignment to be edited and proofread before it is turned in. Who else is going to help unless it's your peers?

Extra research task

Ask students to research areas of the world that experience extreme weather conditions such as hurricanes, flooding, drought, extreme cold, etc., and find out what design solutions people have invented for coping in the area. You might have them think about how housing or roads might have to be adapted for the area or if special structures are put in place to help protect cities.

UNIT 3 THOUGHT

Reading	Skimming Understanding vocabulary from context
Vocabulary	Collocations: noun + verb
Writing	Summarizing
Grammar	Adverb clauses of reason and purpose

Background information

The picture on page 27 shows a hood filled with electrodes for measuring brain activity. The brain gives off electrical signals that can be visually recorded as an electroencephalograph (EEG). This can give researchers an idea of which parts of the brain are active during different tasks such as listening, drawing, or remembering. EEGs are commonly used for medical diagnostic purposes, as well as in brain study research.

Discussion point

Lead in to the topic by referring to the picture on page 27. Ask: *What does it show? Where might the picture have been taken? Why are all of the electrodes red except for one, which is yellow? Do you think the hood is supposed to go on a human or a robot? What do you think the purpose of the electrode-filled hood is? How do you think it connects with the unit title 'Thought'?*

Ask students to discuss the questions with a partner. In the feedback session, you could write up the lists on the board from question 1. For question 2, you might ask students if they have any good tips for remembering things that they could share with the others. When they have finished, have several pairs share their ideas with the whole class.

Vocabulary preview

Ask students to identify the form of all the words in the box before attempting the exercise, and make sure they are correct. Note the endings of the words that can give clues to the form. Ask students to label the nouns as either count or non-count—this will also help them to complete the exercise. You could point out that, although it looks like *study* or *evidence* makes sense in sentence 1, only *evidence* fits grammatically because there is no *a*, indicating that a non-count noun is needed. Ask students to add the words to their vocabulary notebooks with their own sentences as examples.

ANSWERS

1 Evidence	5 efficiency
2 study	6 concentrate
3 accuracy	7 expand
4 performance	8 challenge

EXTENSION ACTIVITY

Ask students to make a word family chart in their vocabulary notebooks and find other word forms for each of the vocabulary words.

READING 1 Is your memory online?

Word count 436

Background information

It is thought that we can store four to seven items in our short-term memory. One strategy for increasing short-term memory is to chunk items together. So, for example, if you want to learn a phone number (e.g. 414 4787996), you would learn the area code (414), then the prefix (478), then the final digits (7996). In this way, you can memorize a longer chain of numbers.

However, this short-term memory only lasts for about 20 minutes, so if the item is to be remembered properly, it needs to go into long-term memory. Strategies for long-term memory recall include link and story methods, the Roman room system, and sensory mnemonics.

One of the keys to long-term memory storage that seems to span all memory methods is making a connection to something that is already known. This is important for students because if they want to remember new vocabulary or new information, they need to connect with it in a personal, meaningful way. New vocabulary, for example, is learned better if students write their own sentence using the word, or connect the sound of the word with a similar word they know in another language.

Studies on sleep have shown that getting enough sleep improves memory. It is during sleep that we consolidate information learned in the day. So students who stay up late and get up early are not helping themselves!

Lead in to the topic by writing on the board: *memory, remember,* and *remind*. Ask students how the three words are connected (*remember* and *remind* are actually the verb forms of *memory*), and where memory takes place (in the brain). Because students sometimes get them mixed up, you could spend some time looking at how *remember* and *remind* are used:

remember is something you do yourself (*I remembered the word*) while *remind* is something you do to someone else (*I reminded him of the word*). Ask them what they think the reading title means.

Before you read

Be sure to refer students to the *Think about* box first. After students have discussed the questions in pairs, it would be interesting to find out what they use the Internet for and how they use it. The unit 8 *Study skills* section goes into more detail about trustworthy sources and criticality when searching the web, but it's worth going ahead and getting students thinking about whether or not all information on the web is credible.

Global reading

Exam tip

In exams, students will be expected to skim texts to get the main idea. Learning the technique of skimming and learning to do it quickly will help students improve exam scores.

Elicit or remind students of the reading skills learned so far. Compile a list on the board. Ask them if they remember from unit 2 what skimming is. Ask them to read the *Skimming* box. Check for comprehension by asking: *Why should you read quickly when skimming? Why does step 1 look familiar?* (these are the previewing skills learned in unit 1) *Why should you read the first paragraph? What will you find there?* (the introduction, which gives an overview) *Why should you read the first and last sentence of the paragraph?* (this is where the topic and concluding sentences are) *Why should you read the last paragraph?* (it's the conclusion).

It may be useful to point out that these skimming tips highlight the importance of the structure of English writing. It's not just the students who have to write like this, but everyone!

1 Ask students to follow the instructions for exercise 1. Monitor the time limit for them. Ask them to cover the article after one minute. Students may feel frustrated at such a short time limit, but assure them that it is good practice and reassure them that it will take practice to perfect the skill. If they are unable to skim the whole article, then they are most likely not skimming, but scanning, or they are getting stuck on unknown words. For more practice, they can skim articles of their choice at home.

2 After completing the exercise, ask students to read the article again to check their answers. Find out how well they understood the main idea by skimming.

ANSWERS
1 the Internet   4 different
2 information   5 research
3 experiments

Close reading

The *Close reading* activity introduces students to the idea of note taking from an article. Ask students if they ever take notes when they read and how they take notes. Then ask them to read and correct the errors in the notes.

ANSWERS
1 Psychologist at Columbia University conducted ~~3~~ 4 experiments
  Aim: How is the Internet changing ~~students~~ memory?
2 Experiment: people typed words into a computer
  1ˢᵗ group: knew computer wouldn't save information
  2ⁿᵈ group: knew computer ~~would~~ wouldn't save information
  Result: ~~1ˢᵗ~~ 2ⁿᵈ group remembered the info better
3 Experiment: gave people info to remember and where to find the folder with the information on the computer
  Result: later, people remembered the location of the info better than the ~~name of the folder~~ facts
4 Transactive memory: we ~~forget~~ remember where to find the information we need
5 Conclusion: because of the Internet, our transactive memory is becoming ~~weaker~~ stronger

EXTENSION ACTIVITY

Ask students to evaluate the layout of the notes in the exercise to see if they have any suggestions for improving them (indenting, underlining, use of color, using shortened forms of words, not using sentences, etc.). Ask them to improve the notes on the article. This could be done on transparencies or big sheets of paper and shared with the rest of the class.

This article has two clear examples of transitional sentences that are worth pointing out to students so that they can start thinking about them for their own writing. Paragraph 3 begins *In another experiment …*; paragraph 4 begins *This is called …* These sentences link back to the previous paragraphs, so they are good transitional sentences. They help hold the article together and make it cohesive.

Developing critical thinking

Ask students to give some concrete examples in their discussions. Also, monitor to see if each individual is contributing equally. If the tally system from the last unit worked, ask students to do it again. You may need to reshuffle groups to find the best group dynamic. After the discussion, ask students to raise their hands if they think they did more talking than others in the group; then if they did more listening; and finally if they thought they had an equal balance of talking and listening. This will serve to raise student awareness of their participation in groupwork.

Extra research task

Ask students to research memory improvement techniques. (Try searching using *memory improvement tips* or *memory improvement techniques*). The Mind Tools website has some excellent tips and ideas for practice games. Tony Buzan's mind mapping site is also very useful.

READING 2 How does the brain multitask?

Word count 685

Background information

The definition of *multitasking* is "the activity of doing more than one thing at the same time" (www.macmillandictionary.com). The term first came into use in 1966 and originally referred to computers performing several tasks at once. When the term became used for humans is difficult to pin down, but psychologists have been studying "divided attention tasks" since the middle of the 1800s. Other, older multitasking-related expressions include: *You can't dance at two weddings; You can't walk and chew gum at the same time* (both meaning that you are unable to multitask); *to have your fingers in too many pies*; and *juggling too many things* (meaning you are multitasking too much); and Lewis Carroll's expression *The hurrier I go, the behinder I get* (which might support the argument that multitasking is inefficient).

Dave Crenshaw (author of *The Myth of Multitasking: How 'Doing it All' Gets Nothing Done*) distinguishes between switch tasking and background tasking. Switch tasking is the type of inefficient multitasking discussed in *How does the brain multitask?* Background tasking is doing routine tasks that don't require thinking, such as watching TV while ironing. He says this type of multitasking is very efficient.

It is often said that women are better at multitasking than men, and there is some evidence to support this. MRIs have shown that the corpus callosum—the area of the brain that is responsible for synthesizing information between the left and right side of the brain—is wider in women than in men. This could mean that the two sides communicate more efficiently and would support the theory.

To lead in to the topic, you could tell a story about your own hectic schedule and things you have to do at the same time in order to elicit the theme of multitasking, or you could use the picture on page 31.

Before you read

Give students a minute to think about their examples, then ask them to share their ideas in pairs. Ask two or three students to share with the whole class.

Global reading

1   Remind students of the skimming skills by referring back to the *Skimming* box on page 28. Set the timer for one minute for them to skim, and when the time is up, ask students to cover the page so they are not tempted to look back at the article for the answers. Keep reassuring them that skim reading takes practice.

ANSWERS
1 F   2 T   3 F   4 F

2   Ask students to answer the questions. You could let them do this in pairs if they are having difficulty recalling the information.

ANSWERS
1 electronic media
2 to view the brain in action

Close reading

1   Students will be relieved to know that they can spend a little more time on the *Close reading* section, but tell them that it is quite important that they don't use any dictionaries or translators (the next skill is understanding vocabulary from context). If it makes them feel more comfortable, ask them to underline words they don't know so they can look them up later if needed.

Ask the students to read the questions first, and then scan for the answers. Allow no more than ten minutes for the exercise.

ANSWERS
1 One group were given one task, but the other group were given two tasks to do.
2 It showed that the brain only works on one task at a time.
3 They used MRI images to monitor brain activity during the tasks.
4 It takes longer to complete each task and more mistakes are made.
5 These tasks require less concentration.

The first thing many students do when they get to an unknown word is reach for a translator. This makes for very poor reading because by the time they have found the word, they have lost their train of thought. Convincing students that they should not do this can be difficult. For very stubborn students, you can bring in a photocopy of the text (or any text) and some black marker pens. You can also use the Digibook text *Time to think* for this activity and use the pen tools built into the Digibook. Ask students to read the text and completely obliterate every unknown word with the marker. Assure them that the original text is still in pristine form in their course book (or that you will give them a clean copy), so they don't need to worry. Once they have done this, ask some general comprehension questions. Most students will be able to answer the questions even if they have many words blacked out. This will serve to illustrate that a text can be understood even if every word is not known.

As a lead-in to exercise 2, ask students what they do when they meet a word that they don't understand. Hopefully, you will have some students who already have good strategies (try to guess, skip it, underline it, etc.). Ask students to read the *Understanding vocabulary from context* box for tips. Afterwards, check that students have understood the word *context* (the words surrounding a word that help to give it its meaning).

2 Give plenty of time for exercise 2 and allow students to discuss with each other if they wish. Assure them that, although they may initially find it challenging, it is an important skill to learn if they want to become good readers. Ask them to write a synonym or definition of each word. Check to make sure no one is using a translator or dictionary!

POSSIBLE ANSWERS
1 describes things that use technology such as laptops, cell phones, and computers
2 television, radio, Internet, etc. (the opposite of "print media")
3 the area in the front of the brain responsible for problem solving, decision making, planning, and emotions
4 at the same time
5 going from one to another
6 reduces
7 a restriction
8 the words of a song

EXTENSION ACTIVITY

At this point in the course, students will have a fairly sizeable bank of vocabulary words, but probably won't be reviewing the ones from previous units. Now might be a good time to start a class vocabulary box, which can be used for review activities so that the words are recycled and, hopefully, moved to long-term memory.

You will need a box and either slips of paper or 3 x 5 cards. Write the vocabulary word on one side with the part of speech, e.g. *vocabulary (n)*, and a definition, synonym, or example sentence on the other. Put them in a box and use them for five-minute fillers or review games. Allow students to access the box if they finish early, or to add vocabulary to it. Encourage students to make a similar box for themselves at home so that they can spend 5–10 minutes per day reviewing vocabulary.

Developing critical thinking

1 Ask students to discuss one or both questions in groups. Then have them share ideas with the class.
2 Remind students of the text *Is your memory online?* Ask them if they think there is a connection between this text and *How does the brain multitask?* Then ask them to discuss the questions. The two questions could be discussed in class by all students, or groups could choose which question to discuss. Alternatively, you could set one of the questions for an online class forum.

EXTENSION ACTIVITY

Ask students to create a poster for the school aimed at younger students. The poster should highlight the reasons against (or for, if they can support their opinion) multitasking when studying. Invite them to use pictures and text, and to draw it by hand or design it on the computer.

Vocabulary skill

Sometimes students' vocabulary use isn't really wrong; it just doesn't sound right. It can be hard for students to understand why, so understanding the idea of collocation is important. If you have a monolingual class and know the language of the students, you could find some examples of collocation in their language to get the idea across that some words just don't sound right together because "it's not the way we say it." If you have a multilingual class, after reading the *Collocations: noun + verb* box you could ask students to think of examples of "words that go together" in their own language.

Introduce the idea of collocation by using a simple example: we would say *a tall tree, a tall person*, but not *tall shoes.* We can say *do homework, do well,* but not *do a mistake.* Ask students why, and elicit or tell them that these are examples of *collocation.* Ask the students to read the definition of collocation in the *Collocations: noun + verb* box. See if they can think of other examples from English or their own language.

1 Before students complete the sentences, point out that more than one answer may be possible, for example, in the tense used.

POSSIBLE ANSWERS
1 conducted; analyzed
2 conducted; analyzed
3 adopted; addressed
4 analyzed; conducted
5 analyze
6 address; adopting

EXTENSION ACTIVITY

Before moving on, it might be worth spending some time trying to learn the collocations. Ask students to draw four word maps in their vocabulary notebooks to record the collocations for each verb, e.g.

Spending some time writing out the collocations will help fix them in students' minds.

Next, give out some cards with all the verbs and nouns on them to each pair of students, and ask them to categorize them without looking in the book. Alternatively, if you have a lot of space, write each of the four verbs onto a large sheet of paper and pin the papers up around the room on different walls. Divide the class into teams and give each team some slips of paper, a different colored marker, and some poster putty. Ask them to write the nouns on the slips of paper (one word per slip). With all books closed, ask the teams to stick their nouns onto the sheets of paper with the verbs they collocate with. The winner is the first team to stick all their nouns in the correct place.

2 This could be done on transparencies or for homework and turned in for checking.

WRITING A summary and a response paragraph

Background information

Writing summaries and responses are common writing tasks in universities. They are used to show that students have understood the key points of lectures and written materials, and that they are able to evaluate what they have heard or read. Summaries generally follow this pattern:

Title of the article (author) and topic

Key points

The author's conclusion (*The author says that …; The author concludes that …*)

Note that first paragraphs are generally introductory, not key, and may not need to be included in the summary. Summaries never use "I."

As a lead in to the section, ask students to work in pairs. Ask them to tell each other about a recent book they have read or movie they have seen. When they have finished, ask them if they described the main plot or details. Normally, they will have just described the main plot unless the details were particularly significant. Next, ask the same pair of students to now say what they thought of the book or movie. When they have finished, tell them that they have just completed a summary response assignment!

Ask students to read what they will learn to do in this section. Find out what they know about summary writing. Ask them to read the *Summarizing* box to see if they were right.

Writing skill

1 Ask students to skim *Is your memory online?* again to complete the summary. Set a time limit of one to two minutes for this.

ANSWERS
1 Is your memory online?
2 memory
3 experiments
4 remember
5 memories

---

2 If you wish, put students into pairs to discuss the questions about the summary. Feed back with the whole class.

3 For the summary, ask students to plan using the questions in the *Summarizing* box to guide them. The summary should be fairly short (50–75 words). For weaker students, provide the following sentence frames:

The article … is about …
Scientists used … to show …
A multitasking study showed that …
The author says that …
Researchers concluded that …
The author believes that …

When marking the summaries, look to see that the students have:

- written the title
- used their own words
- summarized the key points only (no details)
- said what the author says about the topic
- kept to the word limit (too many words probably means they are including unnecessary detail).

POSSIBLE ANSWER
In the article *How does the brain multitask?*, the author explains what multitasking is and discusses recent research about what happens in the brain while we multitask. Research shows that the brain does not actually do two things at the same time, but rather switches quickly between tasks. The brain uses its working memory to store information on one task while switching to the second task. Working on more than two tasks at a time leads to more mistakes. Experts say that it is better to concentrate on one task and do it efficiently.

Grammar

To introduce the grammar, you could start by asking students some *why* questions in order to elicit some reason and purpose clauses, e.g. *Why do people multitask? Why do you search the Internet? Why do architects design buildings that are attractive?* Put some of the responses on the board. Ask students to read the *Grammar* box to see if any of the ways they expressed reason and purpose were the same as the ones listed. Ask students why the first two sentences contain commas, but the third doesn't (in the third the adverb clause is at the end). You may wish to ask students the difference in structure between *in order to* and *so that*, and elicit that *in order to* is followed by the infinitive verb, and *so that* is followed by normal sentence structure (subject, verb, object).

Don't let students get too worried about terminology such as *adverb clause*. The important thing is that they can use the clauses to express reason and purpose correctly. There is no real difference between purpose and reason for the purpose of this exercise, though grammatically the phrases work differently.

1 Point out to students that more than one answer may be possible for some blanks. When the students have finished, check the answers with the class.

ANSWERS
1 so that
2 Because / Since / As
3 because / since / as / due to the fact that
4 because / since / as / due to the fact that
5 in order to

2 Ask students to write complete answers to the questions. Circulate to check they are using correct adverb clauses of reason and response. Have students compare sentences in pairs before feeding back with the whole class.

POSSIBLE ANSWERS
1 As I hope to have a career in international business, it's important for me to be fluent in English.
2 I use the Internet in order to do online research for my classes, and to communicate with friends and family.
3 Sometimes I go to the library and set a time for myself to work without stopping so that I can focus on my studies.
4 While I am doing my homework on the computer, I often have a chat window open and my email open so that I can get messages from my friends. Since it is more fun and easier to socialize than to study, I often end up wasting my time chatting with friends rather than getting my schoolwork finished.
5 I often have good ideas in the early morning, before my day gets started. It's a quiet time of day, and my mind is more relaxed so that it is more open to good ideas. I also get good ideas when I am walking because I allow my mind to wander.

WRITING TASK

Brainstorm

1 Ask students to read the task, and draw their attention to the box that details the audience, context, and purpose of the writing task. Then ask them to read and follow the directions for the response paragraph.

> ### ANSWERS
> He felt much calmer, his concentration was better, and he seemed to be more creative in solving problems. Adverb clause of reason: <u>In order to examine how multitasking may cause stress in my own life</u>, I decided to try the author's no-multitasking experiment. Adverb clause of purpose: It would be interesting to set up a school experiment <u>so that we could learn how other students experience a few days of no multitasking.</u>

Ask students to compare the response to the summary by asking the following questions: *What is different about the response? Why does it use "I"? Does it refer to research? What is the topic sentence? What is the concluding sentence?*

2 Ask students to choose either *Is your memory online?* or *How does the brain multitask?* and to follow the instructions for the task. Point out that they must think about their own opinion and personal experiences of the topic.

Plan and write

Allow plenty of time for the planning stage. Monitor and give help if needed.

Refer students back to the summaries in exercises 1 and 3 in the *Writing skill* section on page 33. Tell them to write a fuller summary for the text they chose, encouraging them to add at least two sentences to the paragraph. Then have them write a response paragraph. The summary should be 65–90 words long. The response should be 120–150 words long.

Share, rewrite, and edit

Ask students to exchange their paragraphs with a partner. Encourage students to use the Peer review checklist on page 109 when they are evaluating their partner's paragraph. Before they feed back, you may wish to point out that not all the items on the list will be relevant in this context, for example, number 2.

Ask students to rewrite and edit their paragraphs. Encourage them to take into consideration their partner's feedback when rewriting.

Use the photocopiable unit assignment checklist on page 90 to assess the students' paragraphs.

STUDY SKILLS Plagiarism

Cultural awareness

The idea of plagiarism can be a foreign and bemusing concept for students of some cultures. In fact, in some cultures, using the words of another writer is seen as honoring that author. Other students simply can't understand what the big deal is. Despite all the emphasis that is placed on avoiding plagiarism, it will take some students a very long time to accept that the practice is viewed negatively in many countries and that it is as serious an issue as teachers make it out to be.

Culturally, one possible reason that plagiarism is so frowned upon is that a high value is put on personal recognition for something that you have done or created. It is the individual who is rewarded for his efforts. If someone copies him without giving him recognition, it is seen as stealing because the words and ideas that the author used are his property. This is what is meant by intellectual property rights. In universities, plagiarism is taken very seriously and can be the grounds for expulsion.

Write *plagiarism* on the board and ask students to read the section entitled *What is plagiarism?* on page 36. Field any questions students might have after reading the section.

Once you have discussed the issues surrounding plagiarism, ask students to read the next sections to find out how to avoid it. Ask them to choose three tips that they find the most helpful for them personally.

Extra research task

Ask students to find an article of interest to them from a newspaper, online source, or magazine. It needs to be 400–500 words long and needs to report on something (not a magazine article giving tips, for example). Ask them to read, summarize, and evaluate the article for an audience of peers. Tell them you will "publish" the best summaries and evaluations in a class magazine for other people which showcases interesting articles for students. You can either "publish" the articles in a shared space on the school website, make copies for all the students in the class, or post them around the room or on bulletin boards outside the classroom.

At the end of this unit, use the video resource *Thought development*. It is located in the Video resources section of the Digibook. Alternatively, remind the students about the video resource so they can do this at home.

Reading	Summarizing
	Identifying steps in a sequence
Vocabulary	American and British English: *have to* vs. *have got to*
Writing	Using sensory details in a narrative
Grammar	Adverbs as stance markers

Discussion point

To lead in to the topic, ask students to look at the picture on page 37. Ask: *What is shown? Where do you think this picture was taken? Why do you think this?* (It shows a pot on a fire. It looks like the Middle East. The man has a covered head.). Brainstorm some uses of fire.

Ask students to read the unit overview box so that they know what they will be learning. At the end of the unit, ask them to re-read it to assess their own learning.

1 Explain to students that there are lots of sayings about fire. Ask them to read and match the expressions to their meanings.

ANSWERS
1 b 2 d 3 a 4 c

Find out if students have any fire expressions in their own language. Ask them to translate and define them for the rest of the class.

2 Ask students to think of a situation in which they would use one of the expressions in exercise 1 (e.g. you might *come under fire* if you plagiarize) and use the expression to explain the situation to a partner (e.g. *He came under fire for plagiarizing someone else's essay*).

EXTENSION ACTIVITY

Ask students to make a poster of one or more fire expressions from their own language. They should write the expression, translate it, say what it means, and give an example of when it would be used. They could also illustrate the poster. These could be displayed around the room.

Vocabulary preview

The vocabulary is presented in the context of a sentence, so in order to practice understanding vocabulary from context (the close reading skill learned in unit 3), ask students not to use their dictionaries for the activity. After they have finished, make sure to cover the pronunciation of each word. You could also ask students to identify the word form and for nouns, if it is count or non-count. Students should write the words in their vocabulary notebooks. One way to record them is to list them with the synonyms from the exercise. The words could be added to the class vocabulary box as well.

ANSWERS

1 a	5 a
2 b	6 a
3 b	7 a
4 a	8 a

READING 1 Feeling the heat
Word count 561

Background information

Many years ago, the threat of fire in cities was a major concern, especially since everyone had to use fire in their homes to keep warm. Chimneys were often made of wood (!), and roofs were often made of thatch (tightly woven straw). But even with the threat of fire, many cities in the U.S. and Europe didn't have organized fire departments. The Great Fire of London in 1666, which started in a bakery and burned over two square miles of the city, finally spurred the city into action, and private fire brigades were set up. However, they only protected the houses that were insured and where "fire insurance marks" were displayed.

Early firefighting methods involved passing buckets of water hand-to-hand from a river or well. Eventually, portable pumps were invented, transported by horse-drawn buggies, and followed by horse-drawn steam engines.

Fire departments as publicly funded services and full-time, publically paid firefighting forces were long in the coming in many countries. In the U.S., it wasn't until the mid-1800s that full-time professional firefighters were employed by the city. Today, the fire department is paid for by city taxes, and full-time firefighters are highly trained and generally earn good salaries. However, the fire department still relies on trained volunteer firefighters to help out when needed.

You could use the picture on page 38 to lead in to a discussion about firefighters. Find out how they are viewed in the students' countries and if they had ever dreamed of being a firefighter.

Before you read

Ask students to work in pairs to discuss the *Before you read* questions. In multilingual classes, pair up students who are from different cultures in order to get different cultural perspectives. In the feedback session, it would be interesting to find out if there are any cultural differences in the perception of firefighting, and how fire departments are staffed and funded in different countries. In monolingual classes, you could have pairs form a group with another pair to compare their lists and discuss any differences.

Global reading

Summarizing was a skill covered in the previous unit as a writing skill and is revisited here as a reading skill. Learning to jot down a quick summary after reading helps consolidate ideas. Being able to put the key points of a text into your own words is an important academic skill because this reflection activates a different part of the brain and deepens the learning.

As a lead-in, ask students to remind you of what they learned about summarizing in the previous unit. Ask them to read the *Summarizing* box to see if there is anything they missed.

Remind students of the previewing and skimming skills they learned in units 1 and 3, and tell them to use these to read the text quickly. Give them a one-minute time limit, then ask them to close their books and answer some questions. Ask: *What is the main idea of the text? What kind of text is it? What are some of the key ideas?*

1 Give the students time to read the text carefully and answer the question. Some students may find this challenging, as they have to summarize the paragraphs in one sentence. You could allow them to do this in pairs.

> **POSSIBLE ANSWERS**
> 1 Most people run away from danger; however, firefighters are an exception.
> 2 Firefighters not only put out fires; they also help educate people in the community about how to prevent them.
> 3 Being a firefighter requires physical fitness, knowledge of the science of fire, and the ability to stay calm under stress.
> 4 Fighting fires can be scary, and some situations are very stressful, but it's a rewarding job.

2 Students work alone to re-read the second paragraph and choose the best summary. In feedback, elicit reasons why it is the best summary.

> **ANSWERS**
> b (The summary is shorter than the original paragraph, expresses the main points using different words, and does not include too many details.)

Close reading

Ask students to read the article again and circle the correct answers. With a strong class, you could see if they can answer any of the questions first before they read it again.

> **ANSWERS**
> 1 a range of situations
> 2 an interview and two tests
> 3 make decisions quickly
> 4 are afraid when they see firefighters
> 5 sometimes feels afraid

Before moving on to the critical thinking questions, students might like to spend some time talking about the text. For example, you could talk about the training and skills required to be a firefighter—are these the same in the students' cultures? You could also ask some or all of the following questions: *What qualifications are required in your country to be a firefighter? Are firefighters and medical emergency services linked in your country? How are fire safety tips taught in your country and/or school?*

> **EXTENSION ACTIVITY**
>
> As a follow-up, you could have students assess the fire protocols for the school, and if they find that there is not enough information for student safety, they could research safety tips and either make posters to put up around the school or create a proposal to present to the school board.
>
> Another idea is to ask students to create a job advertisement for a firefighter based on the information in *Feeling the heat*.

Review the skill of recognizing collocations by asking students to locate the words in the *Academic keywords* box in the text and identify the collocations: *avoid being hurt; an exception to the rule; assess the situation.*

Developing critical thinking

Groups could answer one or both questions. Encourage students to support their opinions with reasons.

EXTENSION ACTIVITY

By now students should be more comfortable working in groups, but if you find that some groups need more encouragement, you could do an activity using a variation of Edward de Bono's thinking hats:

Make a set of six cards or hat-shaped cards in the following colors and with the following information written on them:

White—you are neutral; you like facts and making lists

Yellow—you are positive and optimistic; you like to look for the benefits

Black—you are judgemental and always looking for why something might not work

Red—you are emotional; you make decisions based on feelings and emotions

Green—you are creative; you like to introduce new ideas and possibilities

Blue—you are administrative; you like to think about the steps that are needed to make a decision or do something

Tell students that Edward de Bono researched how to make groups more productive and focused. He developed the idea of the different roles people play in groups and symbolized these roles with different colored thinking hats. Tell them they are going to take part in a discussion, but taking on the role of the thinking hat that you give them.

Divide students into groups of six. Extra students can be observers. Give each student a different colored "thinking hat." Ask them to respond during the discussion from the point of view of the instructions on their card. You could either give them a topic or task (such as planning a study group session), or use the critical thinking questions. After they have had the discussion, ask them how they felt in their role. Find out how the discussion went—was it better managed? Less successful? Find out how different the role they played was from their normal role. Ask them if they felt the task was useful as a way to make group work more productive.

READING 2 Fire in the sky

Word count 507

Background information

Fireworks are used all over the world in celebrations, and in some countries they are used to scare away birds! There are several classifications of firework—from the small fireworks used by individuals to the large ones that are only permitted for use by qualified professionals. Because they are potentially dangerous, fire departments are generally on hand to put out any fires that start.

The chemicals used in fireworks cause the different colors. Copper gives a blue color, and lithium creates red. The different effects—spider, crossette, kamuru, palm-shell—are created by the arrangement of the chemicals in the shell of the firework. The sound effects—whistle, crackle, bang—are also created by the way the shell is packed.

Animals can become very frightened during fireworks displays. Pets can be very distressed, and wild animals may flee in fear—often into the road. Nesting birds are known to abandon their chicks due to the noise of fireworks. Farm animals suffer, too, and there have been reports of farm animals literally being scared to death by fireworks displays. It is for this reason that there is a movement in many rural areas to ban fireworks.

As a lead-in, ask students to look at the picture on page 41. See if they know the term for what is shown—*fireworks* or *fireworks display*. Ask them if they like watching fireworks displays. Find out if anyone has animals that have been affected by displays.

Before you read

Ask students to discuss the questions in pairs. In a multilingual class, it would be interesting to find out what celebrations usually involve fireworks.

Global reading

Ask students to skim the article and tell you what the main idea of it is. Remind them to skim the pictures, title, headings, caption, and first and last sentence in each paragraph. Ask them to read the text again to complete the summary. Encourage them to try to understand words from context, but you could allow monolingual dictionaries if needed.

ANSWERS

Fireworks, also called pyrotechnics, have been used as a form of entertainment for centuries. The first firecrackers were made <u>from bamboo in China around 200 BCE.</u>
Later, between 600–900 CE, <u>Chinese chemists began experimenting with making firecrackers by putting different types of chemicals into tubes.</u>
In 1292, <u>Marco Polo introduced fireworks to Italy.</u>
During the Renaissance, <u>Italians began to make true pyrotechnics. Word spread to other countries, and fireworks became a popular form of entertainment.</u>
By the 1700s in England, <u>fireworks displays became big public events.</u>
Today, <u>fireworks displays may include between 40 and 50 thousand fireworks. They are operated by highly trained professionals using computers.</u>

Close reading

Ask students how the information in the text is organized. Write the word *chronological* on the board, and tell students that *chrono*, like *pyro* from the article, comes from Greek and means *time*, so if something is arranged chronologically, it is arranged in time order (or order of events). Ask students to read the *Identifying steps in a sequence* box to find out what kinds of texts are typically organized chronologically. Ask them to complete the exercise individually, before checking the answers with the whole class.

ANSWERS

1 f	4 a
2 b	5 e
3 d	6 c

EXTENSION ACTIVITY

A timeline is an excellent graphic organizer to use to help students plot the sequence of events in a text. You could ask students to create a timeline based on the information in the article. Encourage them to illustrate the timeline so that they are using more areas of their brain, which will result in deeper learning.

Refer students to the words in the *Academic keywords* box. Ask them to find the words in the text and note any collocations, then add them to their vocabulary notebooks.

Developing critical thinking

On page 108 of the Student's Book is a list of functional language which may help students during their discussions. Ask students to look at the phrases and go through the functions with them to ensure they understand them. Next, drill the pronunciation

of the phrases, or record them so that students can listen and repeat at home. Ask students to choose several phrases (or one phrase from each section) that they want to try to use in the *Developing critical thinking* discussion.

1 Ask students to work in groups to discuss the questions. Some of the critical thinking questions could be discussed in a discussion forum, or in a reflective writing assignment.

2 Remind students of the text *Feeling the heat*. Ask them if there is a connection between this text and *Fire in the sky*. Then ask them to discuss the questions in groups.

EXTENSION ACTIVITY

The media is full of examples of people who are attracted to danger, especially when it comes to extreme sports. Find out if any of your students do any extreme sports or dangerous activities, and see if they would be willing to talk about what they do and why. Other students could devise questions and interview them about their sport.

This would be a good place to use the video resource *Fire and fun*. It is located in the Video resources section of the Digibook. Alternatively, remind the students about the video resource so they can do this at home.

Vocabulary skill

Although American and British English are primarily the same, they do have some differences in grammar, vocabulary, and pronunciation. Usually these differences do not impede conversation, though it may be necessary to ask for clarification. British English would have used *have to* in the past, and British people carried this usage to the colonies. At some point in history, *have got to* came into use in Britain, but not in the U.S., which explains the reason for the distinction today. There is no difference in meaning between the two, and *got* has no additional meaning. Interestingly, it is possible in some regions of the U.S. to hear *I gotta* /ˈgɑtə/, which is the shortened form of *I've got to*.

In American English, *have to* and *has to* are shortened to /ˈhəvtə/ and /ˈhəztə/ in speaking. In British English, *got to* is shortened to /ˈgɑtə/ or even /gɑˈə/ in some regions.

Ask students if they know any differences between American and British English, and brainstorm some ideas on the board. Ask them to read the *American and British English: have to vs. have got to* box and field any questions.

1 Refer students back to the text *Feeling the heat* and ask them to work with a partner to underline all the sentences with *have got to*.

2 Students now work alone to complete the sentences with the correct form of *have got to*. Point out that they should use the contracted form.

3 Drill the pronunciation of the phrases in the *American and British English: have to vs. have got to* box before asking students to complete the statements. To add an element of drama, you could ask students to adopt a British or American accent depending on which form they use. They could even do it in pairs as a guessing game, where Student A says a sentence with either the British or American form, and Student B has to listen carefully and say which it is.

WRITING Narrative essay: A time when you faced danger

Ask students to read what they will learn to do in this section, so that they know what will be expected of them. You may need to pre-teach *narrative* (a story) and *stance* (your point of view). Hopefully, they will ask what *sensory* means, as it would be a great lead-in to the next section!

Writing skill

Ask students what *sensory* means and, if necessary, write on the board the root word *senses* to help clarify. Ask them what they think *sensory details* might be—see if they can give some examples. Ask them to read the *Using sensory details in a narrative* box to find other examples and check their ideas.

There are some useful collocations listed in the box. Spend some time with the vocabulary so that students can get the feel of it. Encourage them to use their monolingual dictionaries to look up the words.

Ask students to read the story and complete the text with the words in the box.

Afterwards, discuss the picture that the writer paints about her hike. How does the choice of language create the mood of the narrative? How does the mood change if you replace *bright, sunny* with *dark, gloomy*, for example? Ask students to play around with the mood by adding different adjectives. Ask students to read their altered narratives to a partner.

Grammar

On the board, draw a stick figure or figure of a person standing. Underneath, write *stance* and ask students if they remember what it means. Ask them how it relates to the figure you have drawn. You could point out that a person's *stance* on an issue could be expressed idiomatically as *where you stand* on an issue. Hopefully, the image and expression will help students remember the word. Ask them to read the *Adverbs as stance markers* box for specific examples of stance markers.

Show the students how easy it is to make a stance marker by writing on the board: *surprising* → *surprisingly*; *honest* → *honestly*; *lucky* → *luckily*. Ask them what the adverbs mean or indicate (the writer thinks it is surprising; the writer is being honest; the writer thinks she/he is lucky).

1 Brainstorm a few more examples on the board before asking students to complete the excerpt from the text.

ANSWERS
1 Naturally
2 Honestly
3 Unfortunately
4 Fortunately
5 Amazingly

2 Ask students to read the narrative, ignoring the blanks. Have them work alone to complete them with a suitable stance marker from the box. Point out that in some cases more than one correct answer is possible, and that not all the stance markers in the box will be used.

ANSWERS
1 Naturally / Obviously
2 Surprisingly / Amazingly / Thankfully / Fortunately
3 Surprisingly / Shockingly / Amazingly / Thankfully / Fortunately / Luckily
4 Thankfully / Fortunately
5 Thankfully / Fortunately / Luckily

WRITING TASK

Draw students' attention to the box that details the audience, context, and purpose of the writing task. Point out that as this is a personal narrative, they will need to use stance markers and sensory details to convey the emotion of the situation. Ask them to read the assignment. If students have never faced a dangerous situation, then ask them to make one up.

Brainstorm

Ask students to use the word map to brainstorm. If this is the first time they have used one, brainstorm some ideas together on the board so they can see how to use it, then allow them to do their own. For advanced students, they could subdivide the word map into senses—auditory, tactile, olfactory, and gustatory.

Plan and write

Students may like to draw a timeline of events before completing the chart in the *Plan* section.

Students should aim to write about 200–250 words, and their narratives should have topic and concluding sentences.

Share, rewrite, and edit

Ask students to exchange their paragraphs with a partner. Encourage them to use the Peer review checklist on page 109 when they are evaluating their partner's paragraph, as well as the questions in the *Share* section.

Ask students to rewrite and edit their paragraphs. Encourage them to take into consideration their partner's feedback when rewriting.

Use the photocopiable unit assignment checklist on page 91 to assess the students' paragraphs.

EXTENSION ACTIVITY

Ask students to type their narratives and "publish" them by making copies for the class to read. You could just make three or four copies that can be shared and read at different times, during recess, etc.

STUDY SKILLS Managing stress

Ask students if they ever feel stressed and if so, what kinds of things make them stressed. Ask them not only about tasks they have to do such as test-taking, but also how the behavior of others can stress them out. Ask them for some ideas of how to deal with stress. Prompt students if necessary (e.g. read a book, take a long bath, drink herbal tea, try to focus on one thing at a time, count to ten, tune out noise, etc.) and write some of their ideas on the board.

If you are able to display the Digibook, ask students to close their books. Put the page-faithful part of the Digibook up on the screen, and cover the headings and subheadings. Write the headings and subheadings on the board, then ask students to read the page, and tell you where each heading and subheading should go. Students can check answers by looking in their books.

Exam tip

The activity above is similar to many exam-type questions in which students have to match headings to a paragraph. To be able to do this kind of task successfully, students need to look for key words in the paragraph that are connected to the topic of the heading.

You might like to try out the daydream or relaxation exercises. Ask students to sit comfortably and talk them through the steps. Another idea would be to put students into pairs. Student A will read, and Student B will try to introduce an element of stress into Student A's reading. Ask Student A to scan the article and find ten ideas for managing stress. Ask Student B to try to distract Student A—by asking questions, counting down the time, telling him to hurry up, etc. Feedback by finding out how Student A felt and if he was able to employ any stress reducing strategies in order to complete the task. Ask students to swap roles and repeat the activity, with Student B finding ten ideas that Student A did not mention.

If you are not able to display the Digibook, give the students some time to read the page more carefully and check any tips that they find particularly useful for managing stress. Also ask them to highlight any tips that they already do. When you feed back with the whole class, ask each student (if possible) to tell you one idea for managing stress that they found particularly useful. If you have a large class, ask students to write the idea down, saying why they thought the idea was useful. Ask students to pick out two or three ideas that they would like to try out in their daily life, and talk to their partner about how they plan to implement it. For example, a student might wish to try to be more organized, so she may get her clothes and papers ready the night before in order to avoid a hectic morning looking for things.

EXTENSION ACTIVITY

An alternative way to do the activity is as a jigsaw reading. Divide the class into five groups and give each group a different section of the page to read. For example, Group 1 reads only the section headed *Stay relaxed*. (The section headed *Relax* might have to be split in half and given to two separate groups.) Their task is to read the section, discuss the ideas, and add more if they like. After all groups have had a chance to discuss the ideas and have taken notes, ask all the students to close their books and regroup so that there is a member of each original group in the new group (each new group has someone from Group 1, Group 2, etc.). Each member should summarize what they read and discussed for the other members. Allow plenty of time for them to share what they have read and any new ideas they came up with.

Movement

Reading	Making inferences
	Using a graphic organizer to take notes
Vocabulary	Collocations: verb + preposition
Writing	Using sentence variety
Grammar	Object noun clauses with *that*

Discussion point

Lead in to the discussion by asking students about the picture on page 47. Ask: *What does it show and what does it have to do with movement?* Elicit *migrate* and show the word forms on the board: *migrate* (verb), *migration* (noun), *migrant* (noun), *migratory* (adjective). You could extend the vocabulary by showing how *immigrate* and *emigrate* use the root *migrate*. Explain that *migrate / migration* generally refers to animals, although it can also refer to people, and *immigrate / immigration, emigrate / emigration* to people.

Ask students to discuss the three questions with a partner. When they have finished, have several pairs share their ideas with the whole class.

Vocabulary preview

Students should try to guess the words from the context when they do the exercise. Ask them to identify the part of speech for each word and to add them to their vocabulary notebooks.

ANSWERS

1	d	5	f
2	c	6	h
3	a	7	g
4	b	8	e

EXTENSION ACTIVITY

When you have finished the vocabulary preview, stage a quiz: ask students to close their books and find a partner. Call out the synonym for each word from the exercise and ask the pairs to write down the vocabulary word. Ask pairs to swap papers and go over the answers. The winning pair is the one who got the most correct.

In another lesson, focus on spelling: play *Hangman* or write up the vocabulary words with the vowels missing. Ask students to complete the words by adding the vowels.

READING 1 Invasive species you should know
Word count 588

Background information

Accidental introduction of a species is only one way that new plants, animals, and insects are brought into another country. Some species are introduced intentionally as in the case with rabbits in Australia or Kudzu in the U.S. Rabbits were kept as food, but it is thought that they were eventually released for hunting sport. Kudzu was thought to be a good idea for controlling erosion before it got out of control. There are dozens of examples of species that were introduced intentionally for economic or sporting / recreational reasons. Sometimes species are brought into a country by immigrants who are nostalgic for the plant or animal. Others might be brought in as pets or for someone's garden. Others might be endangered in their native land and introduced into the new environment in the hope that they will thrive. Whatever the reason, importing species is not a problem unless it becomes invasive— when it gets out of control and begins to impact on the native species. This can cost governments billions of dollars a year because of the impact on native species and agricultural products lost.

Border controls are quite strict in most countries, as authorities try to stop the importation of animals and plants that may be detrimental to the country. One example is rabies, which so far does not exist on the British mainland. Strict regulations have been put into place to prevent infected animals from coming into the country.

Before you read

Pre-teach *invasive* (*to invade* is to enter somewhere and cause problems) and *species* (a plant or animal group). Ask students to look at the pictures and say what the general name for both the creatures is (insects). Ask them to identify one feature that all insects share (six legs). Ask them to guess what the pictures have to do with the title *Invasive species you should know*, then direct them to the exercise. In the feedback stage, you could use the Internet to do an image search for some of the insects that students name. Project the images if possible.

Global reading

Ask students to preview the article title, pictures, and headings, and think of one question they want to find out from the article. Then give them three minutes to read the article quickly to find out the main ideas. For the *Global reading* exercise, they complete the main idea statements with phrases from the box, then match each main idea to the correct paragraph.

> **ANSWERS**
> **2** a ALBs have been carried by cars and trucks in the U.S.
> **3** b Red imported fire ants came to the U.S. from South America.
> **5** c It's important to learn to recognize invasive species.
> **1** d Many invasive species are introduced into new habitats every year as a result of global trade.
> **4** e RIFAs can move their colonies quickly and easily.

Close reading

You could introduce the idea of inferring in a dramatic way. Come into the classroom shaking an umbrella as if shaking off the water, or walk in fanning yourself with a fan as if you were hot. Ask students to say why they think you are shaking your umbrella or fanning yourself to get them making some guesses. You could then point out that what they are doing is making inferences based on evidence. Tell students that we make inferences all the time in daily life.

Ask students to read the *Making inferences* box. Elicit other times when we might infer things.

> **Exam tip**
>
> Making inferences is a common reading exam task which contrasts with the kind of task where information is either *yes, no,* or *not given,* or *true, false,* or *not given.* Inferring questions requires the student to "read between the lines" to draw conclusions or make assumptions about the text.

Ask students to work alone to find the statements and circle the inferences. In feedback, encourage students to say how they made the inferences.

> **ANSWERS**
> **1** a **2** b **3** a **4** b **5** a

Developing critical thinking

Remind students of the phrases on page 108 of the Student's Book. Ask them to choose several that they would like to use in today's discussion. Tell them to put a check next to any they use.

In order to avoid students simply filling in the chart on their own and not discussing, ask one person in the group to be the writer. For the second question, ask students to be sure to give reasons.

> **ANSWERS**
> **1**
>
> | Asian longhorned beetles | Red imported fire ants |
> |---|---|
> | wooden crates on ships | soil in ships |
> | not very easily | easily |
> | it doesn't | attacks people |
> | yes, but very expensive | no |
>
> **2** Red imported fire ants are the most problematic because they can attack people and sting. They can also move around easily and multiply quickly, and are impossible to get rid of.

> **EXTENSION ACTIVITY**
>
> Ask students to discuss any other invasive species (insects, animals, or plants) they know about. If they don't know about any, ask them to do some research to find out. Ask them to prepare a short, one-minute presentation about the species: what it is, where it is from originally, where it has "invaded," and how it got there. This will also help in the critical thinking discussion later in the unit.

READING 2 How do animals navigate?

Word count 659

> **Background information**
>
> The study of animal navigation has been a popular topic since scientists discovered that they use various methods for plotting their course. But how do they track them? Traditionally, scientists used signs such as nests, footprints, droppings, claw markings on trees, and other signs to track animals. Now, with new technologies, scientists can get more accurate data.
>
> Most tracking methods require the scientist to capture and tag the animal with a transmitter connected to a collar, harness, band, or even, in the case of the rhino, by embedding the transmitter into the horn. Sometimes the animal has to be caught again in order to retrieve the data, but to track movement, the data is received by radar or GPS.
>
> Scientists study animal migration in order to find out many things, but one important reason is to learn where they move from and in order to understand how changes in the environment might affect them. It also helps them to understand the species better.

Before you read

Ask students to hypothesize about what is happening in the picture at the bottom of page 50. It shows a sea turtle with a tracking device on its back. Find out if they know why scientists study the migration of sea turtles. Ask them if they know how sea turtles navigate, then ask them to complete the *Before you read* section, first individually, then in pairs to compare ideas.

Global reading

1 Ask students to preview the article using the previewing skills from unit 1. Give them three minutes to read the article before discussing the question with a partner and adding to their notes.

2 In this exercise, students have to make inferences. If necessary, remind them of the inferring skill they learned from *Invasive species you should know* by asking: *What do we do when we infer? Is the information clearly stated in the text?* Ask students to read the instructions and check they understand what to do before proceeding.

ANSWERS
1 d
2 a
3 e
4 b
5 f
6 c
7 Possible answer: If they lose contact with the infrasound waves while they're flying over the ocean, pigeons get lost. / The loud sound of the airplane made them lose their way.

EXTENSION ACTIVITY

Since inferences are not facts, but guesses, when making inferences, tentative language is needed. For example, *This suggests that ... , It could be that ...* Before going over the answers for exercise 2, pre-teach the two expressions above, then ask students to give the answers using this language (e.g. *Sea turtles can read magnetic fields, which suggests that magnetic fields can be felt through water.*). In this way, students get a richer language experience than simply saying the correct letter for each.

Close reading

Students will be familiar with using graphic organizers for brainstorming and writing, but tell them that now they will use them for reading. Ask them why they think using a graphic organizer to take notes from a reading text might be helpful, then ask them to read the *Using a graphic organizer to take notes* box to compare. Show them the chart and ask if anyone knows the word

for that type of graphic organizer. Ask them to read the text again and fill in the chart. You may want to let them use monolingual dictionaries, but encourage them to try to guess the words from context. You could limit the number of words they are allowed to look up to three—the rest they have to figure out or skip.

ANSWERS

	Where do they navigate (to / from)?	How do they navigate?
1 Sea turtles	from place of birth to other areas for food to birthplace to lay eggs	They use a magnetic map, mostly, as well as a sense of smell and sight.
2 Homing pigeons	from an unfamiliar location to their home nest	They use a magnetic map, sights, smells, infrasounds, and they fly over highways.
3 Fruit bats	from their caves to trees	They use visual clues such as lights and hills, magnetic fields, and smell.

Draw students' attention to the words in the *Academic keywords* box and ask them to find them in the text along with the preposition they collocate with (paragraph 2: *a characteristic of something*; last sentence: *depend on something*). Note that *generate* doesn't have a strong collocation. It is passive in the text. This focus will anticipate the verb + preposition vocabulary skill later in the unit.

Developing critical thinking

Cultural awareness

Not every culture shares scientists' desire to protect animals. In fact, some cultures even eat sea turtles. In a multicultural class, there may be a very diverse cultural perspective. In either case, cultural sensitivity may be essential when discussing protecting endangered species. Try to invite impartial, unimpassioned discussion which focuses on evidence and facts to back up any opinions.

1 For the discussion, you could either have all groups discuss both questions, or divide the groups, then regroup them to share their ideas.

2 You may want to discuss the questions in exercise 2 on another day, depending on how ready the students are to continue discussing

issues. Ask students to re-read the text *Invasive species you should know*, using a chart to note the names of the invasive species and how they moved to their new habitats. During their discussion, ask them to extend the chart to include the animals or plants they discuss, and their migration patterns. Refer them to the *Think about* box for ideas. For question 2, you could do a class survey to find out who is good at navigating and who isn't.

Extra research task

If students are particularly interested in knowing more about why sea turtles are endangered, have them research the topic. You could assign a website to each pair (if you key in *sea turtles endangered*, you will find lots of relevant sites), or you could ask students to read one site, such as the Sea Turtle Conservancy, which has multiple subtopics to research—you could assign one subtopic for each pair. Students could then share the information they have found and perhaps make a bulletin board for the school, poster presentation for another class, or video about the subject.

Vocabulary skill

Remind students of the collocations from the *Academic keywords* box earlier. Ask them what came after the verb in the two examples they looked at. Ask them if they think there is a way to predict the preposition, then have them read the *Collocations: verb + preposition* box to find out. After reading, emphasize the importance of learning the verb + preposition and noting it in their vocabulary notebooks. If you are still struggling to convince students of the benefit of monolingual dictionaries over translators, this is further evidence: translators don't give collocations, but a good dictionary does.

1 Ask students to complete the collocations with the correct preposition. If they are having difficulty with any, tell them to do the ones they know first, then go back and do the others.

ANSWERS
1 at
2 to
3 on
4 out
5 in
6 by
7 on
8 of

2 Remind students that they may also need to change the form of the verbs in this exercise. Encourage them to read through the whole paragraph first before completing the blanks.

ANSWERS
1 drawn back to
2 puzzled by
3 rely on
4 figure out
5 in search of
6 concentrating on

3 Put students into pairs to do the task. Encourage them to use the verb + prepositions they have just learned. Monitor to check they are using them correctly.

EXTENSION ACTIVITY

In a later lesson, review the collocations by giving each pair of students a set of cards with the verbs written on and another set with the prepositions written on. Ask them to match them. To emphasize the importance of well-organized vocabulary notebooks, tell them they may look in their notebooks, but not in the textbook.

WRITING Response to an exam question

Ask students to look at the writing topic and what they will learn to do in this section. Ask them what kinds of exams they have taken in the past (in their own language or in English) in which they have had to write a response to a question. Find out if they have any strategies for answering exam questions and tell them they will look at some strategies before they do the writing task, as well as in the *Study skills* section.

Writing skill

To introduce the idea of sentence variety, write the following short, choppy sentences on the board (or use your own ideas) and ask students what they think of your "composition": *Last week was hot. I went to the beach. I stayed there too long. I got sunburned. Next time I go to the beach I'll wear sunscreen. I won't get sunburned.* Ask them how to make it better. Elicit that you need to combine the sentences to make them more sophisticated. Ask them to read the *Using sentence variety* box and tell you what the difference is between a simple, compound, and complex sentence. You may wish to give them the following as an example of a simple sentence that has two subjects: *Destroying all beetles in an area* and *eradicating their eggs, is very expensive and takes time.*

1 Ask students to rewrite the sentences as longer sentences. Because a number of different variations is possible, you may want students to write on overhead transparencies or large sheets of paper to make checking easier. Ask students to look at each other's sentences and check accuracy first. Another way to check answers is to display the

possible answers, and then field questions about any differences. Make sure students understand that there is no one correct answer. Remind them to watch their use of commas.

POSSIBLE ANSWERS

1 He's not fluent in English, but/though he's adept at making himself understood. / Although he's not fluent in English, he's adept at making himself understood.
2 My final destination is Italy, but/although I have to fly to Zurich first.
3 The typhoon was devastating, and many people lost their homes.
4 When/If an animal's habitat is destroyed by human activity, it must search for a new area.
5 Because Costa Rica is famous for its natural beauty and unspoiled environment, recently it has become a very popular spot for foreign tourists.

---

2 Students could work with a partner to rewrite the paragraph if necessary. Point out they do not need to change every sentence.

POSSIBLE ANSWER

Some people can easily find their way in an unfamiliar place, while other people seem to get lost in their own towns. Recent studies have found genetic connections to people's ability to navigate, which may explain why some people are skillful at navigating. Some people are easily disoriented and get lost easily. Studies show that good navigators use landmarks and streets to orient themselves. They use visual geometry. In their heads, they visualize their location in relation to things they see around them. Researchers have found that people with a rare genetic disease can't visually orient themselves. Experts now believe that navigational skills are inherited and that some people lack certain navigation genes.

Grammar

To illustrate what is meant by the object of a verb, write a simple example on the board, highlighting the subject and the verb: *Turtles and birds* lay *eggs*. Ask students what turtles and birds lay. When they say *eggs*, circle it, and tell them or elicit that this is the object of the verb. Then write the example from the *Grammar* box: *I* believe *that the problem is very typical for new students.*

Ask students what *I believe*. The answer is the whole of the rest of the sentence: *that the problem is very typical for new students.* Point out that it is a very long object! Circle it as you circled the object in the simple example. Ask students if they notice anything about the phrase beginning with *that* (it is a dependent

clause; it has a subject and a verb). Underline the subject and verb (you could also circle the object of the verb in the dependent clause). Ask students to read the *Object noun clauses with that* box.

See if students can come up with more examples of *it* clauses (more examples are given in exercise 2).

1 Ask students to put the words in order to make sentences. When they have finished, check the answers with the class.

ANSWERS

1 It is clear that many animals travel great distances during migration.
2 It is a fact that animal migration is often interrupted by human activities.
3 It is obvious that each year many animals must migrate to find fresh sources of food.
4 It was widely believed that migrating nocturnal bats were blown to the island of Hawaii in a storm.
5 It has been shown that oil pipelines interrupt the migration routes of caribou in Canada.
6 It is a fact that each year 5 billion birds migrate from North to Central and South America. / It is a fact that 5 billion birds migrate from North to Central and South America each year.
7 It has been reported that some migrating birds can fly without stopping for 50 to 60 hours.

---

2 Point out that students can either use the words in the box to complete the sentences, or their own ideas. Ask them to check each other's sentences for accuracy and ask you if there are any disagreements. Ask several students to read their sentences to the whole class.

WRITING TASK

Exam tip

Students can lose marks (or fail outright!) if they fail to answer the exam question, even if their composition is perfect. This is often referred to as being "off-topic." Stress the importance of identifying exactly what information the exam question is asking for. Encourage students to use graphic organizers to plan so that they ensure they answer the question fully.

In exams, understanding what it is that students have to do is another key issue. For example, an exam question asking students to *describe* something would be written differently from a question asking students to *comment on*, *compare*, or *analyze* something. If you are preparing students for an exam, you might want to spend some time talking about what exactly is required.

Brainstorm

1 This section will help students to analyze the exam question and think of ways to make the response more sophisticated. For question 1, ask students to map out the information required: they could use a word map or a chart for the five things required. Then, ask them to read the paragraph and write the information the writer included about each of the five. They will notice that the writer didn't include all the required information, so even though the paragraph is good, it would lose marks for not answering the exam question fully.

> **ANSWERS**
> 1 Five pieces of information should be in the answer. The writer didn't include information about why the habitat is suitable.
> 2 The kudzu is an invasive species of plant that has spread …
> The problem was that it grew too fast.
> 3 There is good variety. There are two very short sentences. (*The problem was that it grew too fast. It spread out of control.*)

2 Ask students to read the exam questions and choose one to answer. Ask them to use a graphic organizer to map out what the exam question requires.

For the second topic, discuss what the exam question means when it states … *if possible* and *You may wish to* … Explain that these are suggestions, but following them may increase their score on an exam.

You may wish to do the brainstorming in class, then set the research for homework. If your students lack research skills, you could take the whole class to the computer lab or library so that they can get help from you if needed.

Plan and write

The *Plan section* could be done for homework or in class as part of the writing.

As this is the halfway point of the course, you may wish to do this writing assignment as a formal, timed composition in class. Ask the students to do the research and outline plan before the day of the timed writing. Allow them to bring in an outline only, and check each student's outline prior to setting the timer. Allow monolingual dictionary use. Give students 30 minutes to write the paragraph, then collect all the paragraphs for grading.

Students should aim to write 150–175 words. Even if you do not do a formal timed writing, you could time the students to give them practice at writing under timed conditions.

Share, rewrite, and edit

Ask students to exchange their paragraphs with a partner. Encourage them to use the Peer review checklist on page 109 when they are evaluating their partner's paragraph, and also refer to the exam question to make sure all the required information is included.

Ask students to rewrite and edit their paragraphs. Encourage them to take into consideration their partner's feedback when rewriting.

As students may need more research in order to answer the exam question completely, you may wish to assign this for homework.

Use the photocopiable unit assignment checklist on page 92 to assess the students' paragraphs.

> **Extra research task**
>
> Give students another exam question to research, and write: *Research how scientists track a specific animal or insect. Discuss ways of capturing the animal (e.g. by net, tranquilizers, etc.), methods of tagging (e.g. bands, tags), and methods of tracking (e.g. via radio or satellite). Include what the scientists hope to achieve by tracking the animal.* You may need to pre-teach some language to get them started: *electronic tags; archival tags* (which log data over time); *transmitter; signal.*

STUDY SKILLS Strategies for writing timed essays

If you decide to do the writing as a formal, timed assignment in class, you may want to do the *Study skills* section first. Alternatively, use the timed assignment to raise any issues about time organization that the students might have had when writing.

Getting started

Ask students to discuss the questions. Invite them to add any more things they find challenging if relevant.

In the feedback session, reassure students that it is normal to feel stressed, but that with practice, it will become easier.

Scenario

Ask students to read the scenario, and think about what Jun Ho is doing right and wrong. You could ask them to highlight these in different colors. Have a discussion after the reading to compare ideas.

> **POSSIBLE ANSWERS**
> This is what Jun Ho is doing right: he includes examples or details to support his opinion; he leaves time at the end to check his spelling and grammar. This is what he is doing wrong: he doesn't carefully review the exam question; he starts writing his answer without gathering and organizing his main idea and support; he writes without stopping, thinking that writing more is better than writing well.

One thing that many students do is write out the essay fully in a messy form, then try to copy it more neatly. This is a bad strategy because inevitably, they do not have time to copy their essay. In exam situations, no time is given for copying. You could highlight this problem to re-emphasize the importance and purpose of careful planning.

Consider it

Ask students to read the tips and follow the instructions. They could put a check next to the tips they find easy to follow and a star ✳ next to the tips they need to improve on. Note that number 3 mentions thesis statements. You may wish to tell students that these will be covered in unit 6.

Over to you

Have students discuss the questions with a different partner.

At the end of this unit, use the video resource *Our journey, our dreams*. It is located in the Video resources section of the Digibook. Alternatively, remind the students about the video resource so they can do this at home.

UNIT 6 DISEASE

Reading	Increasing reading speed Distinguishing fact from opinion
Vocabulary	Words with Greek and Latin origins
Writing	Thesis statements
Grammar	Passive modals: advice, ability, and possibility

Discussion point

Ask students to look at the picture on page 57 and describe it. If necessary, use the following questions to prompt them: *What is happening in the picture? Where do you think they are? Why are the people crowded around so close to the woman? What else can you see?* Put any new vocabulary on the board (e.g. *mask, cap, cables, stretcher*). Ask the students to say how the picture relates to the unit title.

You could teach or elicit the word forms *disease* (n) and *diseased* (adj), and common collocations with the noun form: *to catch / have / suffer from / transmit / prevent / eradicate / diagnose / chronic / communicable / infectious / fatal / rare / congenital / preventable disease.*

Pre-teach *medical technology* and *treatment* by putting the words up on the board as word maps and brainstorming some ideas for what each might include, e.g.

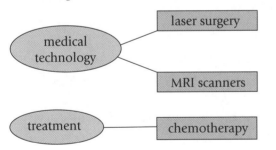

Refer students to the unit overview box, which they can refer back to at the end of the unit to check and see if they have learned the concepts.

Students may need some help with questions 1 and 2. Ask them to think of some old-fashioned treatments that modern medicine doesn't use. Refer them to the board where the ideas from the brainstorm are. For question 2, ask them to focus on what the technology is used for.

The focus of the unit is on disease, so before you start, you may wish to get students interested in the theme by using the video resource *Pills*. It is located in the Video resources section of the Digibook. Alternatively, remind the students about the video resource so they can do this at home.

Vocabulary preview

Ask students to identify the word forms for each of the vocabulary words and the word form required in the blank in each sentence.

ANSWERS

1 precise	5 diagnosis
2 resolve	6 symptoms
3 widespread	7 genetic
4 application	8 disorders

READING 1 Long-distance care

Word count 447

Background information

Telesurgery, or remote surgery, uses a combination of highly developed robotics, advanced communication technology, and management information systems. A robot surgical system will consist of one or two arms (controlled remotely by the surgeon), a master controller, and a sensory system giving feedback to the surgeon. Despite the advantages of telesurgery, it is still not widespread because of a lack of governmental support, as well as a number of practical issues that still need to be resolved (such as the need to make global equipment compatible). It also still requires an anesthetist and back-up surgeon in case of problems with the robot. Nevertheless, despite this, some scientists are trying to develop robots that would be able to perform surgery without any human intervention at all.

Before you read

To lead in to the topic, ask students to speculate on what they think the title *Long-distance care* means. Refer them to the picture on page 58 and ask the following questions: *What is it a picture of? Is it different from what you would expect an operating room to look like? What is different?* Ask them to discuss the *Before you read* questions with a partner. Refer them to the *Think about* box for ideas.

Global reading

Exam tip

In an exam, reading quickly and effectively can mean the difference between finishing or not, so it is important for students to learn strategies for increasing their reading speed. Students need to be able to read as quickly as they can while maintaining comprehension.

Background information

People can learn to read faster by using some techniques developed in the 1950s. Techniques include reading groups of words rather than individual words, using a finger to guide the eyes quickly along the line, avoiding saying the words aloud, and skim reading. Speed reading has been employed by U.S. presidents (Kennedy and Carter), and there is even a speed reading competition. Good speed readers can read thousands of words per minute. Speed reading comes at a price, though. Comprehension can be low. It is important to know when it is useful to read quickly and when slowing down is a better strategy to ensure good comprehension.

Ask students if they think they are fast readers or not and elicit why they think it might be good to be able to read quickly. Ask them to read the *Increasing reading speed* box to find four useful strategies for faster reading.

Point 4 may need additional explanation: some parts of the text can be read more quickly, while other parts containing details that are important may need to be read more slowly. For example, students may read the topic sentence and concluding sentence of a paragraph more slowly, but the actual paragraph more quickly. Key facts may be read more slowly. It is largely up to the reader to decide what information needs more attention.

1 Give students one minute to read *Long-distance care*. Before they read, make sure they understand the task and that they should stop reading when you tell them. Time one minute, then ask them to mark where they got to and complete as much of the chart as they can.

2 Now ask students to read the whole article again and complete the rest of the chart.

ANSWERS

A definition of telesurgery: The doctor is not in the operating room, using a robot and a computer to perform the surgery.
History: First performed in 2001: Dr. Jacques Marescaux in New York City performed gall bladder operation on a woman in France.
Advantages: can be used in places where access to medical care is limited, or travel is difficult; accuracy
The future of telesurgery: training surgeons in developing countries, treating injured soldiers on battlefield, conducting surgical procedures in space

EXTENSION ACTIVITY

As an alternative or follow-up, find out how many words per minute the students are reading and see if they can increase their speed over the next five units. Divide students into pairs. Student A is in charge of keeping time. (Most students in the class will have a stopwatch function on their cell phone, but if not, ask Student A to look at the clock.) Student B should read the text as quickly as possible using one or two of the strategies listed. When Student B has finished, Student A should note the time it took. To find out reading speed, divide by the number of seconds and multiply by 60. For example, 545 words ÷ 165 seconds = 3.30 words per second. 3.30 × 60 = 198 words per minute. Students then swap roles. A good reading speed to aim for is 250 words per minute.

Close reading

If you feel that students need more support with understanding the article, do the following *Extension activity* below before completing the summary.

EXTENSION ACTIVITY

Write the following incorrect statements on the board. Ask students to read the article again and correct them.

1 Telesurgery is more common than traditional surgery.
2 The surgeon must be in the same hospital to perform surgery.
3 Telesurgery helps people who live near larger hospitals.
4 Accuracy is a problem with telesurgery.
5 The first telesurgery was performed from another room within the same hospital.
6 It is unclear whether telesurgery will be used in the future.

ANSWERS

1 Telesurgery may someday be more common than traditional surgery.
2 The surgeon can perform surgery from a hospital far away.
3 Telesurgery helps people who live far from larger hospitals.
4 Accuracy is a not a problem with telesurgery.
5 The first telesurgery was performed from a hospital 6,230 kilometers away.
6 Telesurgery will be used more often in the future.

Ask students to complete the summary using their own words as much as possible. Remind them about plagiarism and tell them this activity is good practice for paraphrasing skills.

Developing critical thinking

For question 1, students have to use inferring skills to decide what the author's views are. Encourage them to give reasons for their opinions, pointing out where in the text they think the author expresses his or her views.

For question 2, ask students to suggest what kind of graphic organizer would be appropriate for organizing their ideas here (e.g. a Venn diagram). Ask them to use one when they list the similarities and differences, and advantages and disadvantages. Refer them to the ideas in the *Think about* box before they start.

READING 2 Do we know too much?

Word count 539

Background information

Beyond the basic understanding that traits can be passed from one generation to the next, people didn't really have an understanding of genetics until after Gregor Mendel in the 1800s. Mendel did experiments on pea plants, and, in a nutshell, discovered that some genes were recessive and others dominant. His discoveries were the key that posthumously opened the door to the study of genetics.

Today, gene technology has so many wider applications. Screening for the potential to develop certain diseases is just one of them. Scientists can now predict if a child is likely to develop hereditary diseases, and conditions such as obesity, asthma, Parkinson's, and even some types of cancer. However, finding that a child is at risk of certain diseases raises ethical issues. If the disease is not preventable or curable, what is the purpose in finding out the risks?

Many are worried about discrimination based on genetic screening. So far, in most countries, the ethical issue of denying employment or medical insurance is a worry rather than a reality. However, there is some evidence that people have been discriminated against in Australia. According to an article in *The Age* (http://www.theage.com.au/national/genetic-health-tests-lead-to-discrimination-20090309-8tb6.html), there have been as many as 11 cases of discrimination based on genetic testing, from denial of medical insurance to denial of income protection insurance. It is clear that the ethical issues surrounding gene technology will need to be discussed and legislated in years to come.

Before you read

You could lead in to the topic with a personal anecdote about who you resemble in your family and by asking students about themselves. Ask students why we sometimes look like members of our family in order to elicit *genetic* (*genes*). Make sure students know what *genetic traits* means (aspects of one's personality or physical appearance) before asking them to discuss the *Before you read* questions. Refer them to the *Think about* box for their discussion.

Global reading

Ask students to read the article, then answer the questions with a partner. You could do another timed reading to see if students can improve their speed.

ANSWERS
1 patients who are displaying symptoms of diseases or who have already been diagnosed with certain diseases
2 four: newborn screening, diagnostic testing, carrier testing, and predictive testing
3 hair or tissue from inside a person's mouth
4 researching a family history and identifying criminals

Before the next section, you could ask the students why they think the author has chosen the title *Do we know too much?* Ask them what the title suggests the view of the author might be. Explore the text for other evidence of the author's viewpoint.

Close reading

Cultural awareness

What is a fact and what is an opinion can be controversial, especially when the issue is based on belief. Some cultural sensitivity may be needed when discussing this.

Many students can find it difficult to decide if something is a fact or an opinion. Getting them to notice the difference and to notice when a writer is being subjective is a crucial step in developing critical reading skills. It is very common for writers to present something as fact when it is, in fact, opinion. It is also common for writers to present "facts" that have no supporting evidence.

One writing strategy authors use to avoid citing the source of information is to use terms such as *many*, *a lot of*, or *few* to state a fact rather than giving a statistic. Compare *Seventy-five percent of students do assignments on time* with *Many students do assignments on time*. The first sentence is clearly a fact, though we need to know the source, otherwise it is plagiarism. The second is stated as a fact, but since there is no statistic, the source is not required. We might, however, question the validity of the information; you could say that it is an opinion masquerading as fact. When in doubt, look at the supporting evidence.

To lead in to the discussion, write a couple of facts and opinions on the board, and ask students to tell you which is which. Ask them to say how they know which is fact and which is opinion, then ask them to read the *Distinguishing fact from opinion* box to find the definition and examples of each. Check they have understood by asking all or some of the following questions: *What is the main difference between a fact and an opinion? What words are used in opinions? Which part of the sentence "A shocking 16.3% of Americans are without health insurance" is fact and which is opinion? Can you give me another example of an opinion presented as fact?* The Digibook has more practice on distinguishing fact from opinion.

Refer students to *Do we know too much?* again and ask them to find the numbered statements 1–6. Tell them to decide which are facts and which are opinions. Put students into pairs to discuss their answers before checking the answers with the whole class.

ANSWERS
1 O   2 F   3 O   4 O   5 F   6 F

Developing critical thinking

SUPPORTING CRITICAL THINKING

Critical thinking is as much about exploring your own views on an issue as it is about exploring another person's argument. In fact, the latter can lead to more informed views. The critical thinking skills in this section are of both types. In the first two questions, students are asked to look for information from the article, and then use the information as the basis for thinking about the issues further. In the second set of questions, students are asked to give opinions, but to think back to the information in the articles in order to substantiate them.

1   For question 1, ask students to summarize the information in a chart. Make sure they realize that *pros and cons* in this exercise mean the same as *positive and negative aspects*. You might want to get feedback on question 1 before moving on to question 2.

The information for question 2 could also be summarized in a chart, or students could use a word map. An alternative way to set up question 2 would be to divide the class into four groups and ask each group to deal with a different type of genetic testing. Ask them to report back to the rest of the class in a mini-presentation.

2   Remind students of the text *Long-distance care*. Ask them if they think there is a connection between this text and *Do we know too much?* Then ask them to discuss the questions. These questions are fairly profound, so you might want to leave plenty of time for their discussion, or ask students to think about them beforehand. You might assign the second question as a follow-up discussion for the class discussion forum.

Vocabulary skill

Remind students that prefixes (and suffixes) are parts of words that cannot stand alone, but are added to a root word to form a new meaning. Refer them to the *Words with Greek and Latin origins* box to find out where many scientific and medical words come from in English. After reading, check that they understand that the word parts listed are prefixes and that they come before a root word.

1   Ask students to work alone to match the prefixes in the first column with the meanings on the right.

ANSWERS
1 c   2 d   3 a   4 b   5 f   6 g   7 e   8 h

2   Students complete the sentences with the words from the *Words with Greek and Latin origins* box.

ANSWERS
1 cerebral
2 cardiologist
3 antianxiety
4 ambiguous
5 optician
6 autobiography
7 psychoanalyist
8 neurological

EXTENSION ACTIVITY

Ask students to find one more word that begins with the prefixes listed. They can use their monolingual dictionaries. In this instance, a paper-based book will be better than an online dictionary, because the page will contain a series of words. Note that some words may seem to have a prefix, but upon closer inspection, it isn't a prefix. For example, the word *ambition* looks like *ambi + tion*. In this case *ambi* is the root of the word, not the prefix. Students will need to look at the meaning rather than just copying down any word.

WRITING Persuasive essay: A health recommendation

Ask students to read about what they will learn to do in this section. Give lots of examples to teach the word *persuasive* and its other forms (*to persuade; persuasion*). Make sure they know what a *recommendation* is (a suggestion or piece of advice).

Writing skill

Thesis statements are an essential part of an academic essay. Students who find them challenging to write are often unclear in their mind about what they really want to say. What is expected of a thesis statement can vary across disciplines. However, the basic tenet is the same: a thesis should be the overall point that a writer is trying to make. Although there are different ways to write theses, this section gives clear guidance for students to follow when trying to write their thesis. The guidelines will help students clarify what they are trying to write and what evidence they will use to support their view.

Find out if students have heard the term *thesis statement* or if they have ever had to write one (you may wish to remind them that they were mentioned in the *Study skills* section of unit 5). You could tell them that the word *thesis* is from Latin, which borrowed it from Greek. Originally it meant *to lay (something) down*, so they could think of a thesis as laying down their main idea. Ask students to read the *Thesis statements* box, and check they understand the three parts of a thesis statement by asking them to identify them in the example sentence. Note that the order can be switched around:

main point
[to stay healthy and prevent disease]

opinion
[The best ways]

how to plan to support it
[a good diet, exercise regularly, and get regular physical exams]

Ask students to suggest a title for the essay, given the thesis statement (e.g. *How to stay healthy and prevent disease; What you should know to stay healthy and prevent disease*).

To show students how the thesis statement helps to organize the writing, draw a simple outline on the board and ask students to complete it:

Title: _____ (use the one the class came up with)

Thesis: The best ways to stay healthy and prevent disease are to follow a good diet, exercise regularly, and get regular physical exams.

Paragraph 2: _____ (e.g. good diet and exercise)

Paragraph 3: _____ (e.g. regular physical exams)

Remind students that the purpose of the introductory paragraph is to *introduce* the topic. You could draw a diagram on the board of the layout of an introductory paragraph:

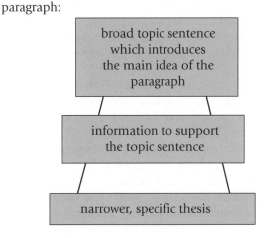

broad topic sentence which introduces the main idea of the paragraph

information to support the topic sentence

narrower, specific thesis

1 Ask students to do exercise 1. Ask them if they think the paragraph starts out broad and then becomes narrower.

> **ANSWER**
> b

2 This exercise revisits the skill of recognizing facts. Three of the sentences are good thesis statements, and the rest are facts. In exercise 3, students practice writing thesis statements. They can use their own ideas or those from the reading texts in the unit. There is more practice with identifying thesis statements in the Digibook.

> **ANSWERS**
> **3** Many health problems can be avoided if people get enough sleep and take steps to reduce stress.
> **5** Older adults should consider the health benefits of switching to a vegetarian diet, including weight loss and a lower risk of heart disease.
> **6** The most important step in preventing disease is for parents to encourage their children to eat more fresh fruits and vegetables, and fewer sugary, fatty junk foods.

3 Now have students rewrite the five facts in exercise 2 as thesis statements.

POSSIBLE ANSWERS

1 People should choose not to have genetic testing because the tests cause unnecessary stress, are too costly, and have poor accuracy rates.

2 People can reduce their risk of heart problems if they avoid stress, get enough rest, and exercise regularly.

4 Employers can offer insurance to both full and part-time employees, if they allow part-time employees to pay a percentage of the cost or select lower-cost insurance plans.

7 Insurance companies should cover telesurgery because it has better accuracy and lower risk of infection than traditional surgery.

8 A vegetarian diet can help people lose weight and improve health; however if they do not follow certain guidelines, health problems can actually arise.

Grammar

It would be beneficial to review the concepts of passive and modal before approaching this section. Write the example sentence below on the board (or use the one in the *Grammar* box). Ask students to identify the subject, verb, and object of the sentence. Write the passive form of the same sentence beneath and draw lines to show how the subject and object swap places.

Surgeons use (telesurgery) to perform remote operations.

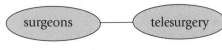

Telesurgery is used by (surgeons) to perform remote operations.

Ask students what the difference is between the two sentences and why we might want to use one over the other (in the first, *surgeons* is the main focus of the sentence; in the second, *telesurgery* is the main focus). Ask them which is active and which is passive, and how they know the difference. Draw students' attention to the *by* in the phrase *by surgeons*, which has to be there unless *surgeons* is also deleted. Finally, show them how it is possible to delete *by surgeons* since it is redundant.

If necessary, quickly review how the passive is formed: (present) *use → is / are used*; (simple past) *used → was / were used*; (present progressive) *is / are using → is / are being used*.

Write the word *can* on the board and elicit that it is a modal. Ask students to give some other examples of modals. Have students read the *Grammar* box to find out what the difference in meaning is between *can / could*, *may / might*, and *should*, as well as how to form the passive with a modal.

You may wish to point out to students that *can* and *could* are both used in the active voice to express ability: *I can see the difference. I could see the difference from the start.* However, in the passive, *could* can express either ability or possibility: *The difference could be seen from the start* (ability); *Telesurgery could be used on astronauts* (possibility).

1 Ask students to read the sentences and check the correct meaning of each passive modal.

ANSWERS

1 Possibility   **4** Possibility
2 Ability   **5** Ability
3 Advice

---

2 Now ask students to rewrite the sentences in the passive. They should leave out the subject where relevant.

ANSWERS

1 All diseases might be prevented someday.

2 The risks of an inactive lifestyle should be considered.

3 Stress can be reduced if people make time to do the things they enjoy.

4 Good health habits can be learned from an early age.

5 Genetic tests should only be taken for treatable diseases.

6 A doctor should be consulted about any health concerns.

7 Memory in older people can be improved through walking.

---

3 For exercise 3, ask students to share their statements with each other, and use peer review to decide (1) if they are correct and (2) whether they express advice, ability, or possibility. Field any questions and ask several students to say one of their sentences to the class.

WRITING TASK

Ask students where they might see a piece of writing on the topic of leading a healthier life. Ask what kind of writing it might be and who might read it. Brainstorm ideas for each question on the board, e.g. where: in a newspaper; a flyer at a doctor's office; in a magazine; in an information sheet for new students; a government report kind of writing: semi-formal but chatty; technical; cautionary who: general public; students; policy makers

Ask the students to read the task, and draw their attention to the box that details the audience, context, and purpose of the writing task. Ask them what kind of tone they will need to use for the essay (semi-formal, as it is an essay giving advice and recommendations).

Brainstorm

Each of the topics relates to ways to lead a healthier life. Ask students to choose one area and brainstorm actions that can be taken to prevent disease or improve health. You could do the first example *changing a habit* together as a model: *stop smoking, drink less coffee, cut out sweets*, etc.

Plan and write

Because students often have trouble writing thesis statements, you might want to ask them to check each other's statements using the three criteria listed in the *Thesis statements* box on page 63. Ask the students to underline or circle the main point, the opinion, and the two examples. Alternatively, you could check them with students as they finish them. Since students have to write three paragraphs, you might ask them to use a graphic organizer to plan, e.g.

Paragraph 1
Topic sentence:
Description of health issue / problem:
Thesis:
Paragraph 2
1st recommendation:
Reasons / examples:
●
●
2nd recommendation:
Reasons / examples:
●
●
Paragraph 3
Conclusion:

Students should aim to write three paragraphs. The first and second paragraphs should be 100–125 words each. The final paragraph may be shorter than the others, but should broadly summarize the issue and give advice.

Share, rewrite, and edit

Ask students to exchange their paragraphs with a partner. Encourage them to use the Peer review checklist on page 109 when they are evaluating their partner's paragraph, as well as the three questions from the *Share* section. You could photocopy the unit assignment checklist on page 93 and ask them to "grade" each other. For the thesis, ask them to point out the main point, opinion, and how it is supported.

Ask students to rewrite and edit their paragraphs. Encourage them to take into consideration their partner's feedback when rewriting. This could be done at home or as a timed writing in class.

Use the photocopiable unit assignment checklist on page 93 to assess the students' paragraphs.

Extra research task

You could ask students to research one of the issues in the reading texts: telesurgery or genetic testing. Then, using some of the information they discovered, they could write a persuasive essay or report about why their local hospital should adopt the practice.

STUDY SKILLS Participating in online discussion boards

Getting started

You may have been using online discussion forums during the course already. In this case, ask the students to discuss how they feel about it. This would be a good opportunity to get student feedback on how the discussion board is used!

If you haven't been using them, then you could refer students back to the article *Discuss it online* in unit 1, which is an online discussion.

Scenario

The scenario brings up a lot of interesting issues that could lead to a fruitful discussion about texting and email habits and expectations, and confidence issues around writing for others. Emphasize that it is the clarity of the message that is important on discussion boards, not perfect style or language. Ask the students to read the scenario, and think about what Fatima did right and wrong.

POSSIBLE ANSWERS
At first, Fatima did not read the instructor's guidelines for online discussion boards. This could have prevented the embarrassing situation. While her response to her classmate was direct, the style she used was too casual, and she did not support her opinion with reasons or examples.

Consider it

After students have read and discussed the tips, find out if they have any to add.

Over to you

If you have not been doing a discussion board with the class, ask them if they would like to set one up. Ideas for how to do this are listed on page 19 of the Teacher's Book.

UNIT 7 SURVIVAL

Reading	Using questions to be an active reader Annotating text
Vocabulary	Prefixes *un-* and *in-*
Writing	Writing about cause and effect
Grammar	Unreal conditional in the past

Discussion point

Lead in to the topic by asking students to describe the picture on page 67. Ask them what they think the person might be carrying, and where he or she is. Ask them how the picture relates to the title of the unit.

Ask students to discuss the questions in pairs. Follow up with a whole-class discussion; find out what the class thinks are the two most essential things to consider when thinking about survival. This could spark some debate!

Vocabulary preview

Ask students to try to figure out the words from the context of the sentences rather than use a dictionary. You may wish to check and drill the pronunciation of *treacherous.*

ANSWERS
1 a   2 b   3 a   4 a   5 b   6 b   7 a   8 b

READING 1 *Adrift*: A book report
Word count 510

Background information

There are lots of tales of people who manage to survive long periods of time adrift in the sea. They all face similar problems: dehydration, exposure to heat and/or cold, sunburn, hunger, sharks, and depression. In many ways, Callahan was lucky because he was in a life raft and at least had some emergency supplies. Not at all deterred from his love of sailing by his ordeal at sea, Callahan continues to sail, design, and build boats. He also writes, and gives lectures and consultations on issues related to sailing, navigating, boat building, and enjoying the sea. You can find out more about Callahan by searching for *Steve Callahan* or by visiting his website at http://www.stevencallahan.net/index.html.

Before you read

Lead in to the topic of book reports by asking students what kinds of books they like to read. Some students may not read books at all, so this might be a good

time to discuss the importance of reading, even if only for language development. Find out if they have ever read or written a book report, then ask them to complete the *Before you read* section. You may need to check that they understand *adrift* (floating on water).

Global reading

SUPPORTING CRITICAL THINKING

Students may think that reading is a passive activity, but it is important to note that good readers are active readers. This means that they ask questions before, after, and as they read—questions about the text itself, the purpose for their reading, the purpose of the author, the type of book, the author's stance, the information in the book, etc. Active reading is a critical thinking skill that can be developed.

Ask students what they do when they read. Many students will think this a funny question and say something like, "I just ... read!" Some students may say that it depends on what they are reading, so you could build the discussion on that. Find out, for example, if students would approach a newspaper differently from a novel or textbook. Find out if they ever ask questions prior to reading, and then ask them to read the *Using questions to be an active reader* box to find four ways in which questions can focus reading.

1 Ask students to read the questions and to think of a sixth question of their own. You may wish to check the questions that students have written before asking them to read the book report. Remind students to read quickly, using the skills learned in unit 6.

ANSWERS
1 *Adrift: Seventy-Six Days Lost at Sea*, Steven Callahan, 1986
2 non-fiction
3 The writer likes to read about true-life survival stories.
4 The story is about a sailor who survives in an inflatable raft for 76 days. It takes place on the Atlantic Ocean.
5 Yes, the writer likes the book because the reader can experience the author's struggles.
6 *Students' own answers*

2 Ask students to now write two sentences to summarize the book. Remind them of the summarizing skills that they learned in unit 4.

POSSIBLE ANSWER
Adrift, by Steven Callahan, is a true story of a man's struggle to survive at sea after his sailboat sinks. The book describes his struggles, both physical and mental, to survive alone on the Atlantic Ocean for 76 days.

Close reading

Tell students they only need one or two words to complete each blank. Check answers before moving on to the second part of the task.

ANSWERS

1 real	8 sinks
2 *Adrift*	9 76
3 survival	10 inflatable raft
4 England	11 salt
5 experienced	12 drinking
6 prepared	13 food
7 large object	14 exercise

Ask students to work individually to make notes on the remaining two paragraphs. Encourage them to try to use their own words in the notes, in order to practice paraphrasing and to avoid plagiarism. Point out they should aim to make the notes roughly the same length as the notes for the first three paragraphs.

POSSIBLE ANSWERS

Paragraph 4
reader experiences Callahan's struggle
suffers from hunger, thirst, and weather
his self-control and problem-solving help him survive

Paragraph 5
author's writing style brings the book alive
strength of spirit and knowledge help him survive
reading the book is unforgettable

EXTENSION ACTIVITY

Ask students to speculate on what they think Callahan pulled out of the boat in his less-than-one-minute rush to abandon ship. Ask them to make a list based on what they have read about how he survived. Ask them if they would have tried to save anything else.

You could also investigate how to make a solar still. Ask students to research how, gather the necessary material, and then try it out.

Developing critical thinking

Refer students to the words in the *Academic keywords* box. Point out that *account* is both a noun and a verb, and they have different prepositional collocations: *to account for someone / something; an account of something.* For *critical*, point out or elicit the following: *to be critical of someone / something; to criticize someone / something.*

Before you group students, you could ask for a show of hands to find out which students enjoy reading or watching shows about people surviving in treacherous conditions. Make sure that these students are equally distributed in the groups so that they can give a personal insight when discussing question 2.

EXTENSION ACTIVITY

This would be a good opportunity to do an extensive reading project with the students, followed by a book report. Extensive reading is important because it improves reading and vocabulary, but also improves motivation. Perhaps the students would like to read the book *Adrift*. Another alternative would be to choose a graded reader for the entire class to read, or suggest readers for each individual to choose from. The benefit of graded readers is that the level can be chosen with just the right amount of challenge to be motivating.

Macmillan has a website which has graded readers listed by level, information about how to use graded readers in class, and even a level test that students can take to find out the best level of graded reader for them (www.macmillanreaders.com). Check with the school library to see if there are graded readers or if the library can order some.

READING 2 A semester on ice

Word count 832

Background information

Blogs (*web* + *log*) and blogging is a popular way to share information and interact online. In the blog *A semester on ice*, the blogger posts his thoughts and experiences, possibly as part of his professional portfolio, or to keep his friends and family back home up to date. Students from the Scottish Association for Marine Science (SAMS) post photos and blog about their third year degree experiences in the Arctic, thus inspiring future students to participate and insuring continued research. SAMS students are working towards creating a sustainable relationship with the ocean and the animals that live there, so their blogs serve an important purpose.

Keeping personal accounts about adventures isn't new. In the past, captains kept written ship's logs, which contributed to the understanding of geography and aided early map-makers. The American explorers Lewis and Clarke described and photographed the landscapes of the Western United States with such detail that it prompted the U.S. government to protect wilderness areas they visited. Early anthropologists wrote copious notes and letters about the cultures they encountered. In fact, Malinowski's notes were so rich that he laid the foundation for future fieldwork methods in anthropology.

It appears that blogging has now taken over what was once done on paper, so we can now find out more quickly about people's research and adventures, maybe prompting others to follow suit.

Ask students to compare and contrast the picture on page 67 to the picture on page 70, then ask them to complete the *Before you read* quiz. See if they know any more facts about Antarctica.

Global reading

Ask students to preview the text and make some predictions about what it will be about. Find out what students know about blogs by asking: *Who writes blogs? Who are they for? Why do people write them? What kind of writing are they?*

Ask the students to read the questions, then give them three minutes to scan the article for the answers. They should try to write the answers in their own words. (Alternatively, ask them to read quickly and note the time it took to read the text. Has their reading speed increased since the last unit?)

ANSWERS
1 Hypothermia is when the body temperature drops to 35°C (95°F) or below, leading to a chain of events that can result in death.
2 lots of clothing, adequate shelter from the weather and moisture, appropriate and sufficient food, and water
3 Questions 2, 3, and 5 are answered in the blog.
4 *Possible answer*: Because the conditions are so treacherous, and they may not have communication, people need to know how to stay safe and warm.

Close reading

Learning to annotate a text is a useful skill for future academic work, especially when writing research papers. Writing a few words in the margin to summarize the topic is especially useful because it trains students to think succinctly about key ideas. Do remind students, however, that they should never annotate in library books!

Some students may already be annotating the texts read in class. Ask them what kinds of information they underline or highlight, or what they write notes about. Ask students to read the *Annotating text* box to find out about annotating and three ways to annotate. Point out that *annotate* has the root word *note* in it, which should help make the word easier to remember.

After completing the exercise, ask students to say which clues helped them match the annotation notes to the paragraph.

ANSWERS
1 f 2 g 3 e 4 d 5 c 6 a 7 b

Developing critical thinking

1 Ask students to discuss the questions in groups. The *Think about* box should help generate some ideas, but you could ask students to do some research if they really don't know. After question 2, you could ask students if they know of any other people who have put themselves into challenging or survival situations, and what they did it for.

POSSIBLE ANSWERS
1 All types of research are done in Antarctica. It's important because scientists can study subjects under very extreme weather conditions, and they can see the effects of weather and the changing climate on animals and resources in Antarctica.
2 He learned about conducting important research in a very remote area. In addition, he will learn about team work, about working in a situation where you cannot easily get replacement parts or assistance, and about a unique part of the world. His unusual experience will help him stand out when he applies for a job.

2 For question 1, students need to look at the text *A semester on ice* to find the four keys to survival. Then they should look at the first reading, *Adrift: A book report* to find out how Callahan dealt with the challenges, inferring information when not stated explicitly.

For question 2, you could divide the class into four groups and give each group one of the situations. To make the task require more team cooperation, limit the number of items allowed to be taken to ten. Groups will have to decide on the essential ten items based on their presentation of good arguments for each. You may need to remind students of the functional phrases on page 108 of the Student's Book. Ask each group to present their list with reasons to the rest of the class, or for large groups, re-organize groups so that there is one person from each original group for the sharing part of the task.

ANSWERS

Keys for survival	Callahan's situation
clothing and insulation	I can infer that his clothing didn't protect him from the sun, heat, cold, and moisture.
shelter	He didn't have protection from the sun or water, or the cold at night.
sufficient food	He didn't have food, but it says that he had a spear for fishing. He must have caught fish.
water	He didn't have enough drinking water, but he was able to devise a still to convert salt water to drinking water.

This is a good place to use the video resource *Adaptation*. It is located in the Video resources section of the Digibook. Alternatively, remind the students about the video resource so they can do this at home.

Vocabulary skill

Review the word *prefix* and brainstorm some examples (e.g. *over* from unit 2). Students may come up with *un* and *in* on their own, but if not, introduce them. Give examples of words which use *un* or *in*: *correct* → *incorrect*; *usual* → *unusual*, and ask students how the prefixes change the meaning of the word. Then, ask them to read the *Prefixes un-* and *in-* box to check and to find other prefixes that do the same. You could check comprehension by asking them to close their books, and testing them by giving a word and eliciting the opposite.

Note that there are some irregular forms, so the rules do not always stand up, e.g. *unregulated, unlock*. It is best to say that the *Prefixes un-* and *in-* box presents a general rule, but that there may be exceptions, so it is always a good idea to check a dictionary. You may also wish to point out that the reason that the prefix changes is largely phonetic. For example, there is no reason not to write *inpossible*, but our mouths naturally turn the *in* to an *im* because of the /p/ sound: both /m/ and /p/ are formed with the lips together. This is called *assimilation*.

1   Allow students to use monolingual dictionaries to find the meaning of the words. When they have finished, check the answers with the class.

ANSWERS

1	inappropriate	9	illegal
2	uncertain	10	immature
3	unconscious	11	unnecessary
4	inconvenient	12	imperfect
5	independent	13	impractical
6	inexperienced	14	imprecise
7	unfortunate	15	insufficient
8	unintelligent	16	irresistible

2   Tell students to read the paragraph first before they complete the blanks. Point out that they will not always need to add a prefix to the word. After you check answers, you could ask students if they have ever seen the show *Survivor* or a similar show. Ask if they would like to go on such a show.

ANSWERS

1	popular	6	independent / intelligent
2	uninhabited		
3	unbelievable	7	inappropriate
4	unusual	8	irresistible
5	intelligent / independent		

EXTENSION ACTIVITY

As a follow-up, ask students to choose ten words and write a sentence or paragraph using the words with the correct prefix. As an alternative, ask them to leave an underlined space where the word should go to make a gap-fill exercise. Ask them to swap papers with a partner so they can complete each other's gap-fill sentences.

WRITING Describing a challenging situation

Ask students to read the section title and think of what *challenging* means in this context (difficult to deal with). Find out what kinds of activities they find challenging. Ask them to read the writing task to find out what they will be learning. Find out what they know about the terms *cause* and *effect*; students often get confused about which is the cause and which is the effect, so it is worth spending some time making sure they get this concept before moving on to the language of cause and effect. Write the following causes and effects from the reading texts on the board to illustrate: *extreme cold* → *hypothermia*; *boat hits something* → *boat sinks*; *self-control* → *maintain sanity*; *one mistake* → *chain reaction of bad events*. You could say that *effect* and *result* are synonyms in this context.

Survival

Writing skill

Ask students to read the *Writing about cause and effect* box. There are a couple of things to point out about the language of cause and effect:

- Which to put first (cause or effect) when using the phrases is tricky for some students, who might write illogical sentences such as: *Extreme cold is the result of hypothermia; He needed to maintain his sanity. Therefore he had self-control.* Students need to understand how the words and phrases relate to cause and effect.

- There is a difference in where the words and phrases are used in sentences: *because, since, as, owing to, because of, as a consequence of* are conjunctions and can be used at the beginning of a sentence or within the sentence: *Because of the cold, he got hypothermia. He got hypothermia because of the cold.* The transition, therefore, needs to go between sentences.

1 If students are having difficulty differentiating between the cause and effect, you could ask them to do this exercise in pairs. When they have finished, check the answers with the class.

ANSWERS
1 C lack of insulation / E loss of body heat
2 E knew how to stay warm in snowstorm / C took a survival course
3 C eating high-energy food / E the body can generate energy
4 C suffering early hypothermia / E the person becomes confused
5 E dressed him in warm, dry clothing / C felt extremely cold
6 C sweating / E skin feels wet and cold

2 This exercise focuses on how the phrases are used in sentences and also the logic of the order. When going over the answers, ask students to say why the deleted word or phrase cannot be used.

ANSWERS
1 A result of
2 As a consequence of
3 enables; creates the skin to feel
4 produces
5 Because of
6 Therefore

3 This discussion gives students speaking practice in expressing cause and effect. You may wish to let them write the sentences first, and/or check answers to make sure students are expressing the causes and effects correctly.

POSSIBLE ANSWERS
1 Walking in the hot sun made me very dehydrated.
2 As a consequence of the fog / it becoming foggy, I got lost in the mountains.
3 Not getting enough sleep can cause people to drive unsafely.
4 We were wearing fluorescent clothing. Therefore, the lifeboat crew saw us very easily.
5 The glow from my cell phone enabled me to find my way through the cave.

EXTENSION ACTIVITY

Play a competitive game in which students have to choose whether or not cause and effect sentences are logical. Create a set of ten cause and effect sentences, some which make logical sense and some which do not.
Either:
1 Stage an "auction" in which teams must compete to buy the logical sentences. (For a step-by-step guide on staging a "grammar" auction, search *grammar auction* on the Internet.)
Or:
2 Give each team the sentences on large cards (one sentence per card), and some Scotch tape or poster putty. Put up two posters on the wall: one which says *logical,* and one which says *illogical.* Ask teams to stick the sentences up on the correct poster. (This could be done as a relay race if you have space and an energetic group.)

Grammar

Cultural awareness

English constructs conditionals through the grammar and tense of the verb phrase, but this is not true of all languages. Mandarin Chinese, for example, uses context and inference in unreal past conditional sentences instead of modals such as *could* or *would.* Because of this significant difference in the way that conditional is formed, some students may have a difficult time understanding the meaning and structure of the unreal past conditional.

To introduce the topic, remind students of *Adrift: A book report.* Review what happened in the story. Then introduce the idea of Callahan's mother, who worries a lot. She knows Callahan is safe, but she worries about what could have happened to him. Ask them to imagine the things that *didn't* happen, but that Callahan's mother might still worry about, e.g. no fishing supplies, the boat not finding him, being eaten by a shark, etc. Write these on the board. Keep emphasizing the fact that these things didn't happen. Ask students to read the *Grammar* box to find out how to talk about what could have happened in the past but didn't.

Ask students to notice how the unreal conditional is formed: *If + had + past participle, modal + have + past participle*.

To check they have understood the meaning, ask them to use the examples on the board to make the sentences that Callahan's mother might have used, and keep checking they understand that it refers to the past and that it didn't happen, e.g. *If you hadn't had fishing supplies, you might have starved!* Ask: *Did he starve?* (no) *Did he have fishing supplies?* (yes) *If that boat hadn't found you, you might have died! You could have been eaten by a shark if you had fallen overboard!* Check that students understand why the grammar is referred to as *unreal conditional in the past* (it didn't happen).

1 Students complete the sentences with the correct form of the verbs. Tell them to use contracted forms where possible.

ANSWERS
1 hadn't sunk; might / would have been
2 hadn't known; couldn't have estimated
3 would have lost; hadn't exercised
4 would have died; hadn't devised
5 hadn't had; wouldn't have had
6 hadn't maintained; might / would have given up

2 To do this exercise, students need to think carefully about the situation in order to come up with a sentence. It is not a simple issue of just using the parts of the sentence given. Students who are not thinking carefully about the situation will come up with sentences such as *If I hadn't crossed the street, the driver might (not) have hit me*. Though grammatically correct, it does not convey the meaning that is intended. You could do the first one together to check that students understand how to approach the exercise.

POSSIBLE ANSWERS
1 If I hadn't jumped out of the way, he would have hit me.
2 If I had reviewed the vocabulary, I would have done better.
3 If I had carefully read my essay before I handed it in, I could have deleted some information.
4 If he hadn't fallen, he wouldn't have broken the chair. If the chair hadn't broken, it wouldn't have bumped the lamp. If he hadn't fallen, he wouldn't have broken his wrist.
5 If it had been windy, I would have been more nervous about my first sailing lesson.

WRITING TASK

Ask students to imagine that they are going to be interviewed for a school newspaper about a dangerous situation (real or imagined) that they experienced in the past. Draw students' attention to the box that details the audience, context, and purpose of the writing task.

Brainstorm

1 Remind students about thesis statements, which they learned about in unit 6. You may wish to point out that although thesis statements are often the last sentence of the paragraph, this is not always the case. Give students a few minutes to read the paragraph and underline the relevant sentences.

ANSWERS
Thesis statement:
After surviving my own treacherous driving experience in the desert, I've learned that driving across the desert in hot weather requires careful planning and preparation.
Cause and effect statements:
Because you will be using your air conditioner to cool the interior of the car, you will be using more gas. You will need to drink more water than usual due to the extreme heat.

2 Most students hopefully will not have been in a dangerous situation, so they will have to imagine one. You could model an example of your own. Show students how to list the details using a time line. Give students plenty of time to think about their situation and details, then get them to tell their story in their groups. Encourage the other group members to listen carefully and ask questions that will help the storyteller enrich the story.

Plan and write

Exam tip
Remind students that careful reading of the instructions is an important exam skill. In their plan, they should make sure that they have included all the points for each paragraph.

As part of their plan, ask students to note down the vocabulary from the unit they plan to use.

You could do the writing task as a timed writing practice in class. Students should aim to write 100–125 words per paragraph.

Share, rewrite, and edit

Ask students to exchange their narratives with a partner. Encourage them to use the Peer review checklist on page 109 when they are evaluating their partner's narrative.

Ask students to check each other's work to make sure that the required information is included before rewriting at home or in class.

Encourage them to take into consideration their partner's feedback when rewriting.

Use the photocopiable unit assignment checklist on page 94 to assess the students' narratives.

Extra research task

Ask students to research the life of a famous explorer or journalist, or someone who has led a dangerous life. They could interview a member of their family if relevant. Ask them to find out about a dangerous experience the person had and to write a "newspaper article" about the experience. They will need to include some background information about the person and why she/he was in the situation.

STUDY SKILLS Using desired outcomes to guide study strategy

The basic idea behind neuro-linguistic programming is that by thinking positively and having clear goals, people will be more likely to achieve those goals. Visualization of the desired outcome and use of positive, "can-do" language are essential. If you can clearly see the goal in your mind and your language is positive about how successful you will be in achieving the goal, then you are more likely to do the things (have the behaviors) that will get you there.

At some point in the course, students may find that their motivation is slipping. Keeping a goal in mind is one way to maintain motivation. Students may not have thought clearly about why they are doing the course or what their desired outcome is. This section will help them think about what they want from the course, which will hopefully kick-start any flagging motivation. It will also be useful for you as a teacher because you may gain insight into your students' goals for the course.

The questions that students are asked to consider when analyzing their desired outcomes require critical thinking and careful thought.

You could begin by asking students why they are studying English (or any other subject) and what their desired outcome is. Ask them how their desired outcome might affect their motivation. Ask them to read the section which lists the three desired outcomes and the differences in how a person is likely to behave with that outcome in mind. Discuss how the motivation of a person with the three different outcomes might differ.

Ask students to read the section *Stating your desired outcomes*. Discuss why they think a negatively formed outcome is "less effective in providing motivation."

Students now write their own outcomes for studying English, using the outcomes given as examples. Once they have written them, ask them to analyze their outcomes using the questions in the *Analyze desired outcomes in detail* section. You may have to pre-teach some vocabulary, e.g. *limiting* (restrictive or constraining), *to put something on hold* (to make something else wait), and *implications* (consequences). Once students have analyzed their outcomes, ask them to discuss them with their partner. Alternatively, they could use a discussion forum or reflective journal.

Reading	Identifying important details
	Identifying sources of information
Vocabulary	Idioms related to success
Writing	Effective hooks
Grammar	Intensifier + comparative combinations

Discussion point

Lead in to the topic by referring to the picture on page 77 and asking the following questions: *What is he doing? What kind of person would want to climb mountains? What do you think drives or motivates a person like that?* Ask students what they think *drive* means in the context of the discussion and picture (the determination to do something). Write some synonyms, word forms, and examples on the board, e.g.

drive = determination, motivation, initiative, get-up-and-go

drive (n); to drive (verb); driven (adj)

What drives a person to climb mountains?

She has a lot of drive and ambition.

He is a driven student.

This would be a good place to remind students that words can have different meanings in different contexts, which is one reason for recording vocabulary (e.g. in a vocabulary notebook) in context and consulting a monolingual dictionary for the word rather than relying on translation.

Be sure to draw students' attention to the goals of the unit. At the end of the unit, ask them to look back at the points to evaluate whether or not they feel they have learned them.

Allow the students to discuss the quotes and their meanings. Encourage them to give reasons for their opinions. Find out if students have any quotes from their culture about drive and ambition. You could ask them to write the quote, and illustrate or explain the meaning. These could be pinned up around the room, then students could walk around reading each other's quotes. This would work especially well in a multilingual class, although could still be done with a monolingual class.

Vocabulary preview

Ask students to try to figure out the words from the context of the sentences. When recording the new words in their vocabulary notebooks, ask students to write the word forms and synonyms or synonymous phrases.

EXTENSION ACTIVITY

The following activity can be used as a vocabulary review. Ask students to draw a 6×6 grid on a sheet of paper. Across the top row, starting with the second column, ask them to write the title of five of the units from the book up to unit 8. Down the first column, ask them to write random letters of the alphabet. Then, give them one minute to fill in the second column with words relating to the unit, but beginning with the letters in the first column. Repeat four more times.

	Thought	Movement
d	decision	destination
a		adept
c	concentrate	characterision
p	performance	
m	mental	

READING 1 Making a difference

Word count 458

Background information

Not only is William Kamkwamba internationally famous, but he has motivated other innovators with his story. Many people have now taken up the challenge of solving local problems with local resources and people. What makes this trend different is that instead of providing people with solutions from outside the community, the emphasis is on working within communities to help people come up with their own workable solutions. This is an enabling approach that is growing in popularity, with organizations and events such as the Maker Faire, which seeks to encourage and celebrate ingenuity.

Before you read

Ask students to discuss the questions, then share their ideas with the whole class. If students struggle with idea generation beyond obvious response topics, offer some prompts. The experience might relate to passing an exam, winning an award, or solving a particular problem. You could give your own example of accomplishment. Talk about factors that might influence the desire to achieve something. These might involve extrinsic motivation, such as the expectation from parents to enter a particular university. Or it might involve intrinsic motivation, such as fund-raising in order to help someone less fortunate out of the goodness of one's heart. Did students consider working toward something that might help others rather than themselves?

Global reading

Ask students to read the questions first, then scan the text quickly to find the answers. Ask them to annotate the text and take notes in their own words. Afterwards, ask students what they think the expression *making a difference* means. It is a common idiomatic expression meaning *to have an effect.* (More idioms are introduced later in the *Vocabulary skill* section.) Ask students what difference William made to his village.

POSSIBLE ANSWERS

1 He grew up in rural Malawi, and lived with his parents and seven sisters in a small clay house without electricity or running water. He had to work on the family farm and study. Life was hard.

2 He had to quit school when he was 13. He wasn't ready to give up his education. He read books from the local library.

3 He saw a picture of a windmill in a library book and began to collect materials. He endured many challenges and failures, but his ambition and determination helped him to continue until he achieved it.

4 With the help of international supporters, his village has clean water, solar lights, and electric power. He was invited to study at Dartmouth College. He travels around the world giving talks.

Close reading

SUPPORTING CRITICAL THINKING

Students need to be able to identify which details are important for them as a reader. The details which are important for one person or in one situation might be different from those of another. It is therefore important for the student to think about their *purpose* in reading. If they are trying to answer a set of comprehension questions, then the important information will be related to those questions. If they are trying to provide evidence to support an argument, then they need to be able to find the details that will support their view. This skill is important as a critical thinking skill and is also important as an exam skill.

You could lead in to the topic of reading for different reasons or purposes by using an example of one text read for different reasons. Ask students if they read the newspaper. Find out why they read it (to find out the news). So for them, the important details are the news items. Ask them if it is important to them who wrote the news article (probably not). Point out that a journalist might find the author very important—it could be a colleague or rival, and they could be reading to find out the kinds of stories she/he is working on. A journalism student might read the article to find out how it is structured, and so would pay attention to the language (transitions, sentence structure, etc.) So, the details that are considered important can differ from person to person.

Ask students to read the *Identifying important details* box for some tips on identifying the important details when they read for exams and courses. Then, ask them to read the statements in the exercise and scan for the details, annotating the text as they read.

ANSWERS

1 work and study
2 kerosene oil is expensive
3 did not get any rain
4 a picture in a library book
5 finally completed his first windmill
6 has clean water, solar powered lighting, and electric power

---

Exam tip

Some exams require students to fill in flow charts or label diagrams based on a text. You could practice this skill by asking students to complete a timeline of events based on the text. Students could do this from memory (then look back to check), or refer to the text as they draw the timeline.

Cultural awareness

A lot of people think that Africa is all rural, or even that it is one country. Especially in the West, audiences are inundated with images of starving African children, so it is hard to visualize Africa in other terms. In fact, Africa is made up of over 50 nations, some richer than others. Although rural areas can be poor, cities are modern. Some nations are involved in wars, but many others are not. Many Africans have never seen a giraffe, an elephant, or a lion. It may be relevant to bring up Africa's diversity if you find that students have a negative or stereotypical view of the people or the continent.

Developing critical thinking

The critical thinking questions could also be done in a class forum or reflective journal.

Extra research task

If you are doing extensive reading as part of the course, students might like to read *The Boy Who Harnessed the Wind*, published by Harper Collins, 2010. You might also like to show the students a video entitled *The boy who harnessed the wind*—this is a short video which can be found on the Internet in which Kamkwamba talks about why he wrote the book. There are other videos about him on the Internet to explore (type *Kamkwamba* into a search engine). Students may find his accent difficult to understand, but do point out that English is one of Malawi's official languages and is spoken with a different accent from that of the U.S., U.K., or Australia.

READING 2 Most likely to succeed

Word count 711

Background information

Definitions of success can vary from person to person and from culture to culture. Jobs, money, and material wealth are all things that many people attribute to success, but others may judge success differently. Success for some could be measured by the number of friends, the level of fulfilment in life, or by how much someone helps others. Some cultures integrate traditional values into their definition of success.

Middle classers refers to the large group of people who are between the working class and the upper class, though this definition can vary in and across cultures. Middle class can be defined by the jobs people do—professional / managerial jobs, for example—the amount of money, level of education, manners, and values and lifestyle someone has. In the U.S. in general, middle classers are people with higher education in professional jobs who have a comfortable and secure income.

In the U.S., high school is secondary education from the age of 15–16 to 18–19. Students graduate from high school, and then go on to vocational colleges, work, or university.

Before you read

Begin by focusing on the word *success* and its word forms: *succeed, successful, successfully*. Ask students to discuss the questions, referring to the *Think about* box for ideas. Ask groups to come up with a definition of success that they can agree on (remind them of the functional language on page 108 of the Student's Book that may help them to agree and disagree). Ask all groups to write their definitions onto a slip of paper, which you will collect. Once you have collected all the definitions, read them out one-by-one and ask the class to vote on which definition they think is the best. Alternatively, you could agree that different people have different definitions for *success* and there is no "right" answer.

Before beginning the *Global reading* section, this might be a good time to do another speed reading check. Put students into pairs and ask Student A to time Student B while they read, then have them swap. Ask students if their reading speed has increased or not.

Global reading

Ask students why they think it might be important to know where information comes from. Brainstorm some ideas. Ask them how they know if what they read is believable or not. Finally, brainstorm some reliable sources of information, then ask students to read the *Identifying sources of information* box to find other examples. You may need to pre-teach the verb *to cite* (to use something someone else has said or written to support your own argument), or ask students to tell you what they think it means by referring to the context.

Ask students to underline the places where the writer cites a specific source as they read, then answer the questions.

ANSWERS

1 interview, scholarly journal, popular journal, website
2 interview—quote, advice
   scholarly journal—information about a research study and its results
   popular journal—quote, examples and terms
   website—quote, advice, tips, examples
3 *Students' own answers*

Close reading

Ask students to read *Most likely to succeed* again and to circle the correct information. If you like, you could ask them to see if they can do any of the exercise from memory before reading again.

EXTENSION ACTIVITY

As an alternative way to approach the text (and to practice summarizing skills), do it as a jigsaw reading. Divide the class into six groups and ask each group to read a different section of the text (there are six sections). Next, ask students to form groups so that each new group has at least six students—one for each section. Ask each student to summarize their section for the others, then, as a group, ask them to complete the *Close reading* task.

Developing critical thinking

Cultural awareness

The picture on page 82 could be used to begin a discussion about how different cultures see the process of becoming successful. In English, we say that someone is *climbing the ladder of success*—success is a ladder to be climbed. Perhaps different cultures have different images.

1 Ask students to discuss the questions in groups. For question 2, ask groups to make a list of both the writer's suggestions and their own suggestions.

2 Remind students of the text *Making a difference*. Ask them if they think there is a connection between this text and *Most likely to succeed*. Then ask them to discuss the questions in groups. You could ask half the class to answer the first question, and the other half of the class to answer the second question. In the feedback session, you could ask students to summarize what someone in their group said about each question.

This is a good place to use the video resource *Profiles of success*. It is located in the Video resources section of the Digibook. Alternatively, remind the students about the video resource so they can do this at home.

Vocabulary skill

Students may be hesitant to use idioms because they equate idioms with slang. However, it is important to point out that idioms are not slang and can be used in more formal conversations and writing (although this depends on the idiom—some are more formal than others). The Macmillan online dictionary

(www.macmillandictionary.com) defines *an idiom* as follows:

An expression whose meaning is different from the meaning of the individual words. For example, "to have your feet on the ground" is an idiom meaning "to be sensible."

However, it defines *slang* as:

Words or expressions that are very informal and are not considered appropriate for more formal situations.

Find out what students know about idioms and elicit any they know. Ask them to read the *Idioms related to success* box to find some success idioms. You may wish to reiterate the point that idioms are set phrases which have a meaning that is different from the meaning of the individual words, and therefore need to be learned as set phrases.

1 Ask students to look back at the text *Making a difference* and find the expressions from the *Idioms related to success* box. Encourage them to use the context to match them to the meaning.

2 Ask students to use the correct form of the expressions to complete the sentences.

3 Students work in pairs to identify two more idioms in the sentences in exercise 2. Encourage them to discuss what they mean from the context, without using a dictionary.

Idioms can be hard to get into a conversation. Ask students to work in pairs to write a dialogue using the idioms, then have them perform it to the rest of the class. Check that they have used the idioms correctly and that they are using good pronunciation and natural intonation.

An example dialogue might look like this:

Student A: Hi, what's up?

Student B: I've been accepted to one of the universities I applied for.

Student A: That's great!

Student B: Yeah, but I really wanted to go to the other one. It looks fantastic!

Student A: Well, you know what they say: the grass is always greener on the other side.

Student B: That's true …

WRITING A proposal

Ask students to read the writing task to find out what they will be learning to write. Elicit what a proposal is (a formal plan or suggestion), and discuss who might write one, who they might write it for, and why (for example, an author might write a proposal of a book for a book publisher; a property developer might write a proposal for a building development for the local planning department of a council).

Writing skill

Introduce the idea of a hook—project an image of a hook or draw a hook on the board. Ask students when hooks are used (for fishing). Explain that if you want to catch a fish, you have to hook it, just as if you want to catch a reader's attention, you have to "hook" the reader. Ask students how they think writers "hook" a reader. Brainstorm some ideas, then ask students to read about effective hooks in the *Effective hooks* box to find other ideas. You may need to explain that an *anecdote* is a short story that you tell. The Digibook has more examples of each type of hook.

1   Ask students to work alone to read the paragraph and complete it with an appropriate hook. You could have students compare their answers in pairs before eliciting ideas from the whole class.

ANSWER
A strong statement

2   Put students into groups to choose four ideas and write a hook for each. If you are short of time, you could ask each group to divide into two and to write two hooks each. Encourage the groups to use a different type of hook for each proposal. Circulate and help out if necessary.

3   Invite groups to share their hooks with the class. You can either ask each group in turn to read out their hooks, or you could go through the list of proposals, asking all groups who have chosen a particular proposal to read out their hook, so the class can compare them.

Grammar

Before introducing the intensifier + comparative combinations, you may need to review when comparative adjectives use *-er* and when they use *more / less*. Write some adjectives on the board and ask students for the comparative form. Ask them how they know if it is *-er* or *more / less*. Elicit the rule: one syllable adjectives, add *-er*; two syllable adjectives ending in *-y*, add *-ier*; other two syllable adjectives or adjectives with more than two syllables, add *more / less* + adjective. Explain that, as always, there are exceptions—you may wish to elicit the irregular comparative forms of *good* (*better*) and *bad* (*worse*).

To introduce the idea of an intensifier, compare two products. Think of two products which differ in price and write on the board: (*Product X*) *is more expensive than* (*product Y*). Ask students how much more expensive product X is. If it is not much, elicit and/ or insert *a little / a bit / slightly* to the sentence. If it is a lot, elicit and/or insert *much / far / a great deal / a lot / significantly*. Ask them to read the *Grammar* box to find out what these words are called.

To check students understand the degree of each word, draw the scale below on the board and ask them to tell you where they go on the line:

slightly a little a bit	even	much far a great deal a lot significantly
Less		More

1   Have students look back at the reading texts in the unit to find the underlined examples. There are two from each text.

ANSWERS
Making a difference: even harder, much better
Most likely to succeed: significantly higher, much higher

2 For this exercise, students need to think back to the proposals for projects from exercise 2 in the *Writing skills* section, then use the examples in the box (or their own) to complete the sentences (e.g. *A new recycling center would make recycling less costly.*).

WRITING TASK

Ask students to read the task, and draw their attention to the box that details the audience, context, and purpose of the writing task. Elicit that because it is a business proposal, the language will be formal.

Part of the proposal can be done in groups since proposals are rarely written by one person alone. You could do the brainstorming and planning sections in groups, then ask each individual to write a proposal. The group can then ultimately decide which proposal is the "best" and which they would like to send off.

Brainstorm

If possible, ask students to identify real projects that would help in the community in which they live. You could even send some proposals off to be read by the relevant person at the school or in the town. Making this a real proposal will be more motivating.

However, students don't have to be realistic about the project if they wish to be more imaginative.

Plan and write

Ask students to spend some time thinking about the questions in the *Plan* section. They could do this in pairs or on their own. Make sure they write answers to the questions as this will help them when they come to write. When they have finished, they could share their ideas with another pair to see if there is any more information that they might include.

The writing could be done in class as a timed writing or at home. Be sure to remind students to read the instructions carefully so they know what to include. Students should aim to write 100–125 words per paragraph.

Share, rewrite, and edit

Ask students to exchange their paragraphs with a partner. Encourage them to use the Peer review checklist on page 109 when they are evaluating their partner's paragraph.

Ask students to rewrite and edit their paragraphs. Encourage them to take into consideration their partner's feedback when rewriting. The proposal should ideally be typed and given a title (e.g. *Proposal for a New Community Center in Louisville*).

Use the photocopiable unit assignment checklist on page 95 to assess the students' paragraphs. As a follow-up, you could ask students to present their project ideas and take a vote on the best one.

STUDY SKILLS Selecting and evaluating online sources

Getting started

Ask students to discuss the questions in pairs and then feed back to the rest of the class. Emphasize the fact that not everything on the Internet is true and that students should evaluate sources carefully.

Scenario

Ask students to follow the instructions and decide what Mariana is doing right and doing wrong. They could also annotate the scenario; ask them to use different symbols to annotate the text: one for the things Mariana is doing right and another for what she is doing wrong. Ask students to compare notes and discuss their ideas with their partner.

> **POSSIBLE ANSWER**
> These days, the Internet is the most popular method used for research. Mariana was right to begin with a search term or question. However, when the list of websites opens, she clicks on the site at the top of the list and begins taking notes immediately. Before using a website for research, she should scan its content and make sure it contains what she is looking for. It's best to scan a number of websites to see which ones offer the most useful information. Then, she should check the validity of the sites, making sure they are accurate, use citations, and are written by reliable sources.

Consider it

Ask students to close their books. Write up the numbered headings on the board and ask students to speculate in pairs what information might be included in each section. Then, ask them to read the text to compare. Find out which tips they already follow and which ones they think are useful for them.

Over to you

Ask students to give the questions careful consideration when they discuss them. Ask them to make a list, then compare it with another pair. Ask some groups to share ideas during feedback.

EXTENSION ACTIVITY

Find some examples of reliable and not-so-reliable websites, and display them on the overhead projector to the class. Have the students critique the sites by thinking about the following questions, which you could write on the board: *Who do you think wrote it? For what purpose? Is it trying to sell something or make you believe something? Is it based on (real) research?*

Extra research task

You could set a research task for homework: ask students to go online, and find a website that they think is reliable and one that they think is not. Ask them to write down the url or print out the webpage. Ask them to be prepared to discuss why they think the site is reliable or not. Alternatively, they could discuss their findings in a forum discussion.

UNIT 9 SOUND

Reading	Identifying tone and mood
Vocabulary	Descriptive adjectives
Writing	Using similes and metaphors
Grammar	Cleft sentences with *what*

Background information

Sounds can be described in different ways in English. In this section, the words used to talk about different sounds are introduced. Because of the nature of sound, the words used to describe them can evoke a different sound in the "mind's ear." So, we could talk about the boom, boom, boom of a drum (the low rhythmic sound of a bass drum), or the bang of a drum, or the beat of a drum. Dogs can bark or whine or growl or pant, and cats purr or miaow. Some sounds don't have variations, so the words used to describe them could be considered collocations: the buzz of a bee, the boom of thunder, the crack of lightning.

The other way to talk about sound is through imitation of the sound, or "quoting" the sound. For example, a cat says, *miaow* and a dog says, *woof* (or *bow wow*). Some are the same: a drum goes *bang, bang* or *boom, boom*, and a bee goes *buzz*.

Cultural awareness

Different cultures have different ways to represent sound based on the way that the sound is interpreted within the language. So, for example, in Vietnamese a cat says, *mio-mio* and in French a dog says, *ouah-ouah*. Interestingly, the sound for an owl in American English is *whoo whoo* while in British English it is *twit-twoo* (*twoo* has two syllables). If you have time and a mix of nationalities in the class, you could explore some of these differences. Ask students to draw the animal or object with the words in speech bubbles representing the sounds they make.

Discussion point

One way to introduce the unit on sound is to play some sounds for students to identify. There are several websites where you can type the sound you want to hear, and it will generate a list from the web that you can listen to. They are easy to use and don't require any advance preparation; key in *sound effects* to search.

Use the picture on page 87 to discuss what sound the two hikers must be hearing. Ask: *Is it a loud sound? How could we describe the noise?* (roar, thunder, rumble, etc.) *Could the hikers whisper to each other or would they have to shout to be heard?*

Ask students to discuss the questions. Invite them to make the sounds in the second question to help fix the name of the sound in their memory. Show students how to change the phrases using different word forms, e.g. *He banged the drum. / The drum went "bang!"* (The last sentence is how we would report the sound using *go* as the reporting verb.) You could also introduce some adjectives and adverbs to show students how to make the sound more evocative: *The <u>incessant</u> banging of the drum drove him crazy. The dog barked <u>incessantly</u>.*

You could build up a class "sound bank" during the course of the unit, using images to accompany the sound descriptions on a large poster or bulletin board. Encourage students to explore more phrases and add them to their vocabulary notebooks.

Vocabulary preview

Ask students first to identify the part of speech of each vocabulary word. Point out that *affect, roar, sweep*, and *trouble* can be nouns or verbs (although you may wish to point out that *affect* as a noun is rarely used; *effect* is more commonly used as the noun). Ask them to identify the part of speech needed in each blank. Have them read the paragraph in full and identify that it is in the past before putting the words in. Ask them to add the words to their vocabulary notebooks.

POSSIBLE ANSWERS	
1 affected	5 roar
2 distinguish	6 confused
3 audible	7 swept
4 ceased	8 troubled

READING 1 *The Secret Garden*: An excerpt
Word count 553

Background information

The Secret Garden is a story about a spoiled young girl, Mary, who suddenly finds herself alone in India when her parents die of cholera. Her wealthy uncle agrees to allow her to live with him in Yorkshire. The house holds a secret which the curious Mary discovers.

It's worth noting the time period of the setting: The British Empire was still strong in the early 1900s. Mary's parents would have been in India as part of the British ruling class. They would have had Indian servants, and in the story, Mary is spoiled by these servants because they are afraid of her parents. Large households in Britain, such as Mary's uncle's, would have had dozens of servants, each with their own duties. The grounds around the manor house would have held gardens to support the nutritional needs of the household as well as ornamental gardens.

Before you read

To lead in to the topic, tell students they are going to read a part of a novel called *The Secret Garden*. Ask them to speculate about what *secret* might mean in this context (hidden, not known about). Tell them to think about the questions, write the answers, and then discuss them with a partner.

Global reading

Since this is the first time in the course that students will have read any actual literature, you could spend a few minutes talking about what is different between a novel and an article or book report (lots of descriptions, dialogue, jumps in time reference, you read them differently—you are unlikely to skim or scan a novel, etc.). Ask them to look at the pictures on pages 88 and 89. The picture on page 89 is of the author. Ask them to speculate on when the book was written. You could give them some background information about where Yorkshire is in England and about England at that time in history. Alternatively, save the background information for after the initial reading if you wish. Make sure they understand *excerpt* (an extract).

1 Ask the students to read the excerpt. Give them a two-minute time limit to discourage them from stopping to look up words. Emphasize the need to read for general understanding and to get the "feel" of the reading. Allow them to look back at the excerpt to answer the questions, then check the answers with the whole class. You could point out to the students that the word *wuthering* is a term used in northern English dialects. It is the roaring sound of a strong wind.

> **ANSWERS**
> 1 They are inside a house, sitting by a fire.
> 2 Mary thinks the sound has come from inside the house, down one of the long corridors.
> 3 It was probably the wind.
> 4 The author shows letters missing from words with apostrophes. The author quotes Martha as saying *wutherin'* instead of *wuthering*, and *on th' moor an' wailin'* instead of *on the moor and wailing*.

Ask students to say what the "feeling" of the story is. What gives it that "feeling"? Ask them to read about tone and mood in the *Identifying tone and mood* box. You may need to pre-teach *non-fiction* (factual). Check they have understood the difference between *tone* and *mood* by asking all or some of the following questions: *Which shows the author's attitude towards the topic? Which is used in both fiction and non-fiction? Which word describes the feeling you get when you read the text? How are tone and mood conveyed?*

A graphic organizer might be helpful to use to try to distinguish tone and mood. Draw a Venn diagram on the board labeled *Tone* and *Mood*. Write up the elements of each randomly on the board and ask students to put them in the correct place in a diagram they draw in their notebooks. Note that the overlapping space is what is shared by each:

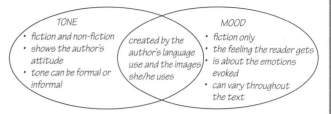

2 Make sure students understand the adjectives before proceeding. Ask them to highlight the parts of the text which show the different moods. Since the next exercise deals with understanding words from context, dictionaries should not be used.

> **POSSIBLE ANSWERS**
> mysterious: 'It must mean that hollow, shuddering sort of roar which rushed round and round the house, as if the giant no one could see were buffeting it and beating at the walls and windows to try to break in.' / 'It was a curious sound—it seemed almost as if a child were crying somewhere.'
> puzzled: 'It was a curious sound—it seemed almost as if a child were crying somewhere.'
> scary: 'It must mean that hollow, shuddering sort of roar which rushed round and round the house, as if the giant no one could see were buffeting it and beating at the walls and windows to try to break in.'
> suspicious: 'There!' said Mary. 'I told you so! It is someone crying—and it isn't a grown-up person.' / 'She did not believe she was speaking the truth.'

Close reading

Remind students of the skill of understanding words from context. Elicit ways to guess meaning without looking up the words. Ask them to do the exercise, highlighting the clues they use to figure out the meaning. Ask them to add the words to their vocabulary notebooks.

> **ANSWERS**
> 1 f   2 e   3 g   4 a   5 b   6 c   7 d

In academia, students may have to read texts that are above their level and will need strategies for coping. However, when choosing a book to read for pleasure (extensive reading), it is important to establish whether or not the book is at the right level of difficulty. A quick way to do this is by using the "five finger rule." It works like this: you begin reading a page. When you get to a word you don't know (or can't figure out from the context), you hold up one finger. Continue to the end of the page. Zero to one finger means the text is too easy; two to three fingers means it is just right; four to five fingers means it is too difficult. Choosing the right level of reading can motivate students to read outside of class.

EXTENSION ACTIVITY

Copy the following exercise onto the board, or make a photocopy for each student or pair of students. Ask them to find each sentence in the excerpt and write what the underlined pronoun refers to.

1 Paragraph 1 <u>It</u> seems to hold many mysteries and secrets. (her uncle's house)

2 Paragraph 1 One night, <u>she</u> is sitting and talking with Martha, a young maid. (Mary)

3 Paragraph 2 … as if the giant no one could see were buffeting <u>it</u> … (the house)

4 Paragraph 5 … as <u>they</u> both jumped to their feet the light was blown out … (Martha and Mary)

5 Paragraph 6 Martha ran and shut the door and turned the key, but before <u>she</u> did it <u>they</u> both heard the sound … (Martha; Martha and Mary)

6 Paragraph 7 <u>She</u> did not believe <u>she</u> was speaking the truth. (Mary; Martha)

For additional practice, the Digibook has two exercises which practice pronouns.

Extra research task

Students might like to read the book *A Secret Garden*. The dialogue is sometimes written in Yorkshire dialect, but students might like to see the difference between the dialects used. Alternatively, you could ask students to research the author to find out where she lived and what other books she wrote.

Developing critical thinking

The students will have to use their inferring skills and some imagination when thinking about the questions. After their discussion in groups, you could talk about how authors of fiction build up suspense. Readers don't always know what is going on and have to keep reading to answer questions they have about the plot. This suspense can make the reader want to read more. Find out if students have read any other books that are full of suspense.

POSSIBLE ANSWER

1 The sound could be a child, or an animal, or just Mary's imagination. Martha may know a secret that she cannot tell Mary.

READING 2 The loudest sound you've never heard

Word count 608

Background information

Infra is a prefix from Latin meaning *under* or *below*, so *infrasound* literally means "below sound." Other words with the prefix *infra* include: *infrared* (light given off by heat which humans cannot see unaided); *infrastructure* (organization, substructure, or foundation of something); and even *infra dig*, meaning *beneath one's dignity*.

The scientific name for the northern lights referred to in the article is Aurora Borealis. They are caused by solar winds colliding with the earth's magnetic field.

A barometer is an instrument which measures air pressure and is used in weather forecasting. When the pressure drops quickly, rain is forecast. Rapid rises indicate fair weather.

Seismographic activity refers to movement of the earth. It comes from the Greek *seismos*, meaning *movement* or *shaking*.

A meteorologist studies phenomena that happen in the atmosphere. The prefix *meteor* comes from Greek, and means *high* or *lofty*.

Before you read

To lead in to the topic, ask students what they think the title means—how can you have a loud sound that you have never heard?

Ask students to read the instructions. Ask them why they think they might have to adjust their reading strategies (e.g. if they know a lot about a subject already, they will be able to read more quickly and perhaps even skip parts of the text). Have them read the questions, then give them 20 seconds to scan the article to find the answers. They should discuss the answers in pairs.

After discussing the scanning questions, you could do a speed reading check. Have them work in the same pairs and ask Student A to time Student B, then tell them to swap roles. Find out if their prediction to the second question in question 3 was correct.

Before you move on to the *Global reading* section, you will need to pre-teach the following scientific terms:

barometric pressure (pressure exerted by the atmosphere as measured by a barometer)

meteorologist (scientist who studies the weather)

seismographic (relating to measurement of strength of an earthquake)

air turbulence (rapid changes in wind speed and direction, and up and down wind currents)

wind turbine (a modern windmill designed to convert wind energy into electrical energy)

You could either just write the terms and definitions on the board, or write the terms on the left and the definitions in jumbled order on the right, and ask students to match them.

Global reading

1 Remind students about tone and mood from *The Secret Garden* before asking them to read and answer the questions.

> **ANSWERS**
> 1 The tone is academic and formal.
> 2 The purpose of this article is to inform, not to entertain like a story. Therefore, the author does not use language to create a mood. It is a science article (i.e. non-fiction).

2 This exercise will help students think about note taking. Have them do the exercise quickly, then check the answers.

> **ANSWERS**
> 5 Infrasound—heard by animals
> 3 Can be created by many natural events
> 6 How infrasound affects humans
> ✗ Can create health problems in humans
> 2 Discovery of infrasound
> 4 Travels through earth and ocean; can be measured
> ✗ Best methods for measuring sound frequencies
> 1 Infrasound—less than 20 hertz very low

Close reading

1 This exercise requires the students to understand details about the text. The sentences are not worded exactly the same as in the text, making the exercise more challenging. When the students have finished, check the answers with the class.

> **ANSWERS**
> 1 F (Scientists can measure sounds that are less than 20 hertz.)
> 2 F (The Krakatoa Volcano erupted in Indonesia.)
> 3 T
> 4 F (Before a volcano erupts, there is a great increase in infrasound.)
> 5 T
> 6 T
> 7 F (Experiments have shown that about 22% of people may be affected by infrasound.)

2 Ask students to use their own words when answering these questions.

> **POSSIBLE ANSWERS**
> 1 Infrasound is a sound that humans cannot hear, but can be measured at 20 hertz or less.
> 2 It broke windows hundreds of miles away and affected barometers around the world.
> 3 Volcanoes, earthquakes, ocean storms, hurricanes, auroras, and air turbulence.
> 4 It increases in frequency and power.
> 5 Elephants use infrasound to communicate with other elephants.
> 6 It can make them feel uneasy.

Developing critical thinking

1 Before moving on to the questions, find out from students how much of what they learned from the article was new information. Ask students to use the ideas in the *Think about* box in their discussion of the questions. Ask groups to compare their lists of pros and cons for question 1. Make sure students give reasons for their opinions in the second part of question 2.

> **POSSIBLE ANSWERS**
> 1
> <u>Pros of hearing infrasound</u>
> We could hear infrasounds made by animals.
> We might be able to predict volcanoes, hurricanes, or storms.
> We could use it for communication.
> It could enhance music concerts.
> <u>Cons of hearing infrasound</u>
> The additional noise would be distracting.
> It might make many people nervous.
> It might block other important sounds.
> We might not be able to distinguish the source of the sound.

2 For the second set of questions, remind students of the story from *The Secret Garden: An excerpt*. Ask them if they think there is a connection between this text and *The loudest sound you've never heard*. Then ask them to discuss the questions.

Vocabulary skill

While descriptive adjectives add interest to a reading text, it is important to point out to students that most academic writing (e.g. essays, reports, and dissertations) tends to avoid the use of descriptive adjectives. Adjectives can show the author's bias, and academic writing is generally impartial and non-biased. Ask students to compare the use of descriptive adjectives in *The Secret Garden : An excerpt* and *The loudest sound you've never heard*. Which text has the most descriptive adjectives? (*The loudest sound you've never heard* has only two: *a mysterious sound; the powerful roars of volcanoes.* They appear to further the writer's point.)

Tell the following story to introduce the idea of the need for more variety and sophistication in adjective use: *Yesterday I went to a nice café and had a nice cup of coffee and a nice slice of cake. The weather wasn't nice, so I sat inside where it was nice. The café was nice—I'd never been there before. I liked the atmosphere—it was nice—and the décor was nice. Even the cups were nice; they had a nice pattern. The waiter was nice, and the price of the coffee was nice. I really had a nice time. I think I'll go there again.* Ask what is wrong with the story and elicit that it only uses one adjective: *nice.* Ask them to read the *Descriptive adjectives* box. Check they have understood by asking them why they should vary the adjectives they use.

1 Ask students to complete the exercise. For the two adjectives that they cross out, ask them to decide which of the senses they would be used to describe (given in parentheses below).

ANSWERS
1 round (sight), juicy (taste)
2 damp (touch), noisy (sound)
3 red (sight), friendly (sight or possibly sound)
4 dark (sight), dusty (touch or sight)
5 delicious (taste), green (sight)

---

2 Point out to students that there may be more than one possible answer for each blank.

POSSIBLE ANSWERS
1 shrill / deafening
2 icy
3 damp
4 golden / bright
5 warm / soft
6 fragrant / delicious
7 soft / muffled

EXTENSION ACTIVITY

As a follow-up, tell the story you used in the introduction to the section again, but ask students to help you substitute more descriptive adjectives.

WRITING A descriptive anecdote

Ask students to read about what they are going to learn. Remind them that they learned the word *anecdote* in the previous unit and elicit the meaning (a short personal story). You can also remind them of the *nice* story you told them in the *Vocabulary skill* section, which is also an anecdote. You may wish to point out that an anecdote is usually about something amusing, frightening, or surprising that happened to a person. Tell them not to worry if they don't know what *similes* and *metaphors* are, as they will learn about these in the next section.

Writing skill

Introduce the topic by writing an example of a simile on the board: *Her smile was like a ray of sunshine.* Ask concept check questions: *Is this a good thing or a bad thing? Was her smile an actual ray of sunshine? Why did I say this, then? Did her smile make me feel like I feel when I experience a ray of sunshine?* Explain this is a simile and that you could say *Her smile was **similar to** a ray of sunshine.*

Introduce a metaphor: *The dark clouds in his eyes told me he was angry.* Ask: *Does he have actual clouds in his eyes? What image am I trying to show with this sentence?* Explain that this is a metaphor, which is more like a painted image or description.

Ask the students to read the *Using similes and metaphors* box to find out other ways to write similes and see other examples of metaphors. Note the construction *as + adjective + as.*

EXTENSION ACTIVITY

Before asking students to complete the exercises, you may need to do some more controlled exercises first. Write the following incomplete sentences on the board and complete them together as a class:

It looks as if …

It tastes as if …

_____ *is like* _____

_____ *is as beautiful as* _____

_____ *is a* _____ (e.g. *My car is a rocket.*)

---

1 Ask students to look back at *A Secret Garden* to answer the questions.

ANSWERS
1 The wind is a giant.
2 The sound was like a child crying.

---

2 This exercise requires students to use their imagination. They should not make the paragraph similar to the original text. Encourage them to paint a different picture with their description. Ask some students to read theirs out or get them to write on transparencies so their paragraphs can be shared.

POSSIBLE ANSWERS
1 the river
2 the sound of the water
3 high
4 it were a train whistle
5 noise
6 a person
7 a train
8 hard to hear
9 real

---

3 Ask students to make sentences using the simile or metaphor. Invite volunteers to share their sentences with the whole class.

Cultural awareness

A lot of proverbs and sayings are similes and metaphors. You could give some common ones in English and ask students to share some from their language:

as stubborn as a mule

as pretty as a picture

to snore like a chain saw

to be like a horse heading for the barn (e.g. ready to get home; not making any detours)

to do something as if your life depended on it

a train of thought

a tempestuous mood

time is money

Extra research task

Ask students to research common similes and metaphors in English. Have them bring them to class and share them in groups. You could make this more challenging by assigning them different topics to find similes and metaphors about, e.g. money, achievement, life, personality, physical appearance, etc.

Grammar

You could introduce the topic by giving an anecdote, emphasizing the underlined words: *At the coffee shop the other day, what I <u>wanted</u> was a chocolate muffin. However, they were out of muffins, so I had a sandwich.*

Write on the board: *What I <u>wanted</u> was a chocolate muffin.* Ask students why they think you said it like this instead of saying *I wanted a chocolate muffin.* Ask them to read the *Grammar* box to find out what kind of sentence it is and why it is used. Check that they understand that cleft sentences are used for emphasis and that the first clause is a dependent clause that functions as the subject: *[What I wanted] <u>was</u> a chocolate muffin.*

1 This exercise helps students see the difference between a question, a regular sentence, and a cleft sentence. When the students have finished, check the answers with the class.

ANSWERS
1 C <u>What he did</u> was measure the low sound frequencies.
2 ✓
3 C <u>What the children love</u> is playing in the water.
4 ✓
5 ✓
6 C <u>What they do</u> is conduct experiments with infrasound.

2 This exercise gives students practice in writing cleft sentences. You could have them compare answers in pairs before conducting a whole-class feedback.

ANSWERS
1 What they decided to do was soundproof the music studio.
2 What I need to do is interview people who work with deaf people for my project.
3 What they want to discuss is solutions to the problems of noise pollution
4 What I felt upset about was that he wasn't listening to what I said.
5 What she always asks for is the quietest room in the hotel.
6 What I love is the sound of waves crashing on the shore.

3 Students complete the sentences with their own information, then compare with a partner.

WRITING TASK

Ask students to read the task, and draw their attention to the box that details the audience, context, and purpose of the writing task.

Brainstorm

1 You could give students some time to think about the topic on their own before putting them into pairs or small groups. Discussing the topics will give students some ideas that might trigger a memory. Give students the option to make up an anecdote, but encourage them to think of a real one if possible. It will make the writing more meaningful and perhaps more useful; many people develop a set of humorous or entertaining anecdotes that they can use in social situations, or within presentations or speeches. Emphasize the need to think of a topic that includes sound in some way.

2 The graphic organizer can help students think of the details that are important in the telling of the anecdote.

Plan

1 Telling the story to a partner can also help to iron out the details. Partners can help each other fill in any gaps in the information in each other's stories.

2 Encourage students to think of metaphors and similes to include. Provide help if needed; alternatively students could use either a printed or online dictionary to find other examples of similes and metaphors.

Write

Remind students about the sentence variety work they did in unit 5. Tell them to aim to write 250–300 words.

Share, rewrite, and edit

Ask students to exchange their anecdotes with a partner. Ask students to check each other's anecdotes for descriptive adjectives, variety of sentence types including cleft sentences, and metaphors or similes. Encourage students to use the Peer review checklist on page 109 when they are evaluating their partner's paragraph. You could also photocopy the unit assignment checklist and get them to assess each other using it.

Ask students to rewrite and edit their anecdotes. Encourage them to take into consideration their partner's feedback when rewriting.

Use the photocopiable unit assignment checklist on page 96 to assess the students' anecdotes.

STUDY SKILLS Using the thesaurus

It is worth spending some time discussing how dictionaries and thesauruses are organized, both because they may be organized differently in different languages (Arabic dictionaries are organized alphabetically by root words for example) and because thesauruses can also differ in organization in English: by category or alphabetically. There are also thesauruses for different specialized fields, and these may be organized in a certain way. You could also point out that word processing programs often have a thesaurus function: in Microsoft® Word, for example, click *Review*, then click *Thesaurus*. You can find online thesauruses as well, for example, the Macmillan online dictionary (www.macmillandictionary.com) has a thesaurus function.

Getting started

Students will no doubt have been using dictionaries throughout the course, but they may not know what

a thesaurus is. If possible, bring some in and ask students to look at them, noting their organization and function. You could also project an online thesaurus (such as the one in the Macmillan online dictionary) or show how the thesaurus functions in a word processing program. Once students know what a thesaurus is, ask them to discuss the questions in pairs.

Scenario

Ask students to read the scenario, and say what Kumar is doing right and wrong. Ask them if they can identify with his problem and to think of suggestions for him.

> **POSSIBLE ANSWER**
> This is what Kumar is doing right: he is sometimes using the dictionary. This is what Kumar is doing wrong: he is not using an English–English dictionary, which would offer more possible word choices; he is not using a thesaurus to find words that may more concisely convey what he means.

Consider it

Ask students to read the tips. You could photocopy the page, blank out the headings, and distribute the copies without headings to the students. Write the headings on the board in random order, and ask the students to read the paragraphs and insert the right heading. This would be an exam-type task.

Another way to handle the text is to put students into pairs, and ask Student A to read tips 1–3 and Student B to read tips 4–6. Then ask them to close their books and summarize what they read for each other.

In the feedback session, go over each point and emphasize point 5—the need to check the exact definition if the word is new.

Over to you

After students have discussed the questions, ask them to draw a word map to summarize their discussion:

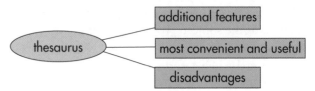

At the end of the unit, use the video resource *Communication*. It is located in the Video resources section of the Digibook. Alternatively, remind the students about the video resource so they can do this at home.

UNIT 10 TOMORROW

Reading	Recognizing the writer's attitude and bias
	Reading statistical data
Vocabulary	Vocabulary for describing trends
Writing	Qualifying statistical data
Grammar	The future progressive

Background information

This unit deals with a number of different charts and graphs, which are used to present different types of statistical data:

Line graphs are used to show trends over time— months, days, years, quarters, etc. Time is the independent variable (i.e. the input or cause).

Pie charts are used to show parts to the whole / percentages; for example, they may show how many people in a given group like chocolate ice cream, vanilla ice cream, or strawberry ice cream.

Bar charts or *bar graphs* are used when there are categories of data, for example, countries or nationalities. They can also show more complex relationships through differently shaded or colored bars. For example, they can show the number of males and females in a number of different countries. These are the independent variables.

Both graphs and charts refer to pictorial representations of data. The terms are somewhat interchangeable, though the term *line chart* is less likely.

Generally, the x-axis (the horizontal line) is used for plotting the independent variable, and the y-axis (the vertical line) is used for the dependent variable (the output or effect). Graphs must have a title and may have a key, especially when different colors are used to represent different sets of data.

The focus of the unit is on the future, so before you start, you may wish to use the video resource *Future friends.* It is located in the Video resources section of the Digibook. Alternatively, remind the students about the video resource so they can do this at home.

Discussion point

To lead in to the unit, ask the students to look at the picture and say how it connects to the unit title. Ask students if, for them, the image represents the future. Here, the image of a road symbolizes the future, but some students may have a different pictorial representation for the future or tomorrow.

Put students into pairs to discuss the questions.

Ask three or four different students to give their predictions for each of the topics for question 1. This is a good opportunity to check that students can use the appropriate future tense, e.g. *Communication will be faster; People will be communicating more through social networks; The economy won't have been sorted out.* You could correct errors as you go without focusing too much on grammar; focus more on the ideas.

For question 2, try to make sure that all topics are covered by at least one pair. Ask each student in the pair to write down the steps. To share ideas, split the pairs up to form new pairs or groups. Ask students to find out and discuss ideas for each of the topics. Alternatively, form new groups of eight, with one student from each topic represented. Ask several students to share ideas with the whole class.

Vocabulary preview

Since this is the final unit, you could find out how independent the students have become in terms of approaching vocabulary tasks. Ask them what they think would be the best way to approach this particular vocabulary exercise: use a dictionary; guess the words from context; use a translator; ask you; look at the word forms, etc. Following the exercise, be sure to check pronunciation and ask students to add the words to their vocabulary notebooks. Ask them to note collocations (e.g. *the notion of; develop strategies; surge in; increase / decrease twofold*).

> **ANSWERS**
> 1 a 2 a 3 b 4 c 5 a 6 a

READING 1 Global graduates
Word count 643

Before you read

Ensure students know the meaning of *global* and *graduates* before asking them to answer the questions. Teach the difference in pronunciation between the verb and noun forms of *graduate*: /ˈɡrædʒuət/(noun); /ˈɡrædʒuˌeɪt/(verb).

You may need to spend some time teaching the students how to read and talk about the chart. The title gives information about what it shows: the university graduation rate for nine countries. The countries are represented along the x-axis, and the percentage of graduates is listed along the y-axis. Check students understand how to read the graph by asking a question such as: *What is the university graduation rate for Australia?*

Global reading

Ask students what strategies they should use to read the article, and how long they think they should take for the first reading (e.g. read the title and headings; look at the image; read the questions first to find out what information they should look for; read the first and last sentences of each paragraph; use chunking or their finger to read quickly; search for key words; skip unknown words). Ask students to complete the sentences in their own words without looking back at the text.

ANSWERS
1 The article discusses trends in graduation rates and international education.
2 According to the article, there has been an increase in the numbers of students graduating from university.
3 Countries around the world are expanding universities and trying to attract more international students.
4 The goals of these countries include bettering their financial situations and attracting talented people to help them compete with other countries.
5 A possible result of these trends is that foreign relations may improve.

EXTENSION ACTIVITY

Since the unit has a strong focus on numbers and statistics, it may be worth spending a little time looking at how numbers are written and pronounced in English. A comma is used to separate the place value in numbers larger than 999, e.g. *2,500*. We use a decimal point in monetary figures and to separate the whole number from the fractional part, e.g. *3.5 million*. This is the opposite in many other countries, where they would write the figure *two thousand five hundred* as *2.500* and the figure *three point five million* as *3,5 million*.

Before moving on to the *Close reading* section, make sure students can pronounce large numbers and years. Write the following numbers and years on the board, and elicit how they are said in English:

2020 = *twenty twenty* or *two thousand (and) twenty*

2011 = *twenty eleven* or *two thousand (and) eleven*

1990s = *the nineteen nineties* (the decade from 1990–1999)

2,500 = *two thousand five hundred* or *twenty-five hundred*

2,500 + = *twenty-five hundred plus* or *two thousand five hundred plus* (meaning *more than 2,500*)

3.5 million = *three point five million*

You could also ask students to highlight any trend language they find in the first paragraph of the text: *… recent positive trends in …* ; *… there has been a surge in …* ; *… have increased nearly two-fold.* Language for describing trends is covered in more detail later in the unit.

Close reading

SUPPORTING CRITICAL THINKING

Strictly speaking, academic writing should not contain attitude and bias. However, some people would argue that it is not possible to remove all bias or evidence of attitude from a text. News and magazine articles as well as web-based articles frequently contain bias. It is an important critical thinking skill to be able to recognize the signs of attitude and bias in order to objectively assess the information given in the text.

Remind students about tone and mood from unit 9. Ask them to tell you how the writer expresses tone and mood. Remind them or elicit that mood is only a feature in fiction writing. Introduce the idea of *attitude* and *bias,* and point out that these are other things that the writer can express through language in factual writing. Define *bias* or ask students to look it up (the writer's attitude towards a topic). Ask students in which kinds of writing they think bias is acceptable and in which kinds of writing it is not. Stress the fact that academic writing should be impartial and unbiased. Ask them to read the *Recognizing the writer's attitude and bias* box to find out how a writer expresses attitude and bias. Have students read *Global graduates* again and do the exercise. You could also ask them to underline or highlight language in the text that shows the attitude and bias of the writer.

ANSWERS
1 F (the attitude is optimistic: swelling tide, better still, more peaceful tomorrow, wonderful opportunities, lasting positive effects)
2 F (As expected …)
3 T (it's clear a college education … is becoming more a necessity than a luxury)
4 T (an entire 'Education City', boasting eight international university campuses, all in just one 14 square kilometer area)
5 F (Contrary to past limitations …)

It is clear that the writer is in favor of university education in general and of international higher education. After students have finished, elicit how the language would be different if the writer were against university education (e.g. if he/she were in favor of promoting practical skills courses such as plumbing and building) or against international education (e.g. if she/he felt that countries should only educate their own people). Ask them where they might find an article such as this one, who might have written it, and why.

Developing critical thinking

Question 1 asks students to think about both the pros and cons. You could point out that by thinking about both sides of the issue, they are being more impartial and unbiased. Refer them to the *Think about* box for ideas during their discussion.

EXTENSION ACTIVITY

Depending on time, you could stage a debate with the students. Divide the class into two groups: Group A and Group B. Divide Group A and B into two sub-groups: Group A1, A2, B1, and B2. Group A will debate the first issue: going to university in another country. A1 will debate the pros, and A2 will debate the cons. Group B will debate the second issue: attending an all-English (or other language) university in their own country. B1 will debate the pros, and B2 will debate the cons.

Give the groups time to discuss their ideas, and come up with their arguments and supporting evidence. If there is time, they could do some research. Encourage them to think of the opposite arguments, too, so that they can counter them. During the debate, the group that is not debating should listen to the arguments, and decide which arguments are the strongest and better supported. Vote on the winning team.

NB: Students don't have to agree with the point that they are arguing. Some of the strongest debaters don't actually agree with the point they are debating, but forcing them to see the other side gives them a better perspective and makes them a more successful debater.

READING 2 Career trends

Word count 467

Background information

The reading describing career trends comes from the "white paper" of the organization *Career Thought Leaders'* conference. The organization aims to support both industry leaders and job seekers globally. After each yearly conference, the organization publishes a downloadable summary "white paper" on its website www.careerthoughtleaders.com. (Go to the website and click on the *Findings from 2010 and 2011 Brainstorming events*, or search for *career thought leaders* in a search engine.) The website gives information for job seekers including how to write a résumé for different professions and typical interview questions. There is also a large section on trends.

Before you read

Introduce the topic of career trends by briefly discussing the kinds of careers or school subjects

students think are more popular, and in which areas they think there is more competition for jobs. Next, ask them to read and rank the methods. Ask students how they think people usually get jobs in their countries.

Global reading

As this is the last reading, you could do one final speed reading check. Tell students to compare their speed now with their previous speed reading checks. Ask students to read and answer the questions.

ANSWERS
1 It is an organization's "white paper" / report about a conference. Its purpose is to report findings after a conference discussion about professional hiring practices.
2 university students, job seekers, companies
3 Job seekers will use more technology to make their résumés stand out. Employers will be using social networking sites more frequently to recruit and check out prospective employees.
4 *Students' own answers*

Close reading

Ask students what kind of information charts and graphs give, and elicit *statistical* information or data. Find out how much students know about how such information is gathered.

Before asking students to read the *Reading statistical data* box, check they understand *bar* by asking them to point to the bars on Chart 1 on page 100. You could also check *average* by writing the following ages on the board and asking students to tell you the average age: 20, 30, 40, 50 (answer: 35).

Once students have read the box, check that they have understood the information by asking some or all of the following questions: *Why is it important to notice the extremes—the tallest or shortest bar, for example? What does comparing the bars tell you? Why is it important to look at the change over time and at what point it changed? How can you tell what the average number is? Why is the overall pattern important?*

Students could study the charts in pairs or on their own to answer the questions.

ANSWERS
1 search for available jobs, and find employers and their company profiles
2 submit their résumé to a recruiter
3 walk-ins and career fairs
4 a good résumé, which summarizes the applicant's experience and highlights their most valuable skills
5 health and medical
6 It's approximately 11 times slower.

There are a lot of important points in the article. You could ask students to answer the following questions (in their own words) in pairs:

1 Why are "extras" important to put on a résumé? What "extras" could you put on a résumé?

2 Why might Facebook not be the most ideal way to make contact with employers?

3 How are job searching and hiring likely to change in the future?

4 Why is online privacy an issue?

ANSWERS

1 They get the employer's attention and distinguish a candidate from others. They could include voluntary work, special training, or membership of professional organizations.

2 Because it is not a professional network.

3 Applicants will be including high-tech multimedia features. There will be a greater use of social networking sites by employers to post job openings and check out potential employees, and by job seekers to post professional profiles.

4 It is important for job applicants to try to separate their professional and personal profiles.

Developing critical thinking

Cultural awareness

Although the information in *Career trends* may be true for Canada, the U.S., and the U.K., the trends may not be true for other countries. In some countries, getting a job may be more a question of who you are and who you know—your connections (although this is a topic that may need to be treated with sensitivity as some students may not be willing to admit this). Other countries put a high value on education level and are not as concerned about "extras" as in the countries listed. Find out what students know about job searching, recruitment, and hiring in their own countries. If appropriate, ask them to research the trends in their countries.

1 Ask students to discuss the first two questions and share their ideas with the rest of the class before moving on to the second set of questions.

2 For question 1, ask students to use their own ideas, and ideas from *Global graduates* and *Career trends*. Refer them to the *Think about* box for ideas. For question 2, ask students to focus on the areas of education and employment. You could divide the class in half so that each half discusses

either education or employment. If necessary, ask students to do some research and report back. The questions could also be used in a discussion forum.

Exam tip

Exams often ask students to summarize graphs, charts, and tables, where they are required to include only the most important points and interpret information. To help students complete this type of task, you could suggest some tips for writing chart or graph summaries:

1 Say what the chart shows: *This chart shows the way in which companies recruit new employees.*

2 Interpret information: *It shows that the largest number, almost twenty-eight percent ... The least popular referral method is ...*

3 Group information: *71% of employees are recruited via referrals, online job boards, and professional networking sites.*

4 Compare information: *More companies recruit by ... than ... Over seven percent are recruited through ... whereas only two percent are ...*

5 Estimations are acceptable: *over 70%; less than 1%*
If appropriate for your class, ask students to summarize Charts 2 or 3 on pages 102 and 103.

Students have now learned many academic keywords and other useful words. Ask them to go through their vocabulary notebooks, and label the words *K* for *I know the word* and *C* for *I feel confident about using the word*. If they have forgotten the word, they could put a question mark. This awareness-raising activity could give students a sense of achievement about what they have learned during the course. It could motivate those who haven't learned as much as they feel they should have to perhaps spend more time reviewing vocabulary. If you have been keeping a class vocabulary box, ask students to spend some time with the cards reviewing the words.

Vocabulary skill

When summarizing a chart, students often make the mistake of trying to report every single line or bar. Instead, students should aim to focus on noticing what is essential or interesting about the data, and reporting that. NB: The Digibook exercises provide more work on trend language.

To lead in to the exercises, ask students whether they think career opportunities are going up or going down. Ask them if there is another way to say *going up* or *going down*. Ask them to read the *Vocabulary for describing trends* box to find out more ways to talk about trends.

1 Students decide whether each word describes an upward or downward trend. They can use a dictionary, but encourage them to try without one.

> **ANSWERS**
> 1 D 2 D 3 D 4 D 5 U 6 U 7 D
> 8 U 9 U 10 U

Once students have completed the exercise, ask them to categorize the words as *big change*, *small change*, or *neutral change* (big change: *dive, plunge, skyrocket, soar, spike*; small change: *dip*; neutral change: *decline, decrease, grow, increase*).

2 Ask students to identify the three different types of chart shown in exercise 2. The first is a line graph showing a trend over time. The second and third show trends using a bar chart. The fourth uses pie charts to show parts to the whole. It is possible to discuss the trend by comparing the two pie charts.

> **ANSWERS**
> Chart 1: spiked; dipped; skyrocketed
> Chart 2: decline; grow; increase
> Chart 3: decline; dive; rising
> Chart 4: surged; rise; an increase

3 Ask students to look back at the charts in *Career trends* and write a sentence about each one, using some of the words and phrases from exercise 1.

WRITING A report on a current trend

Ask students to read about what they are going to learn and write about. Don't explain or let them look up *qualifying* until after they have read the writing skill section.

Since the writing task requires students to research some statistics which may take some time to find, you could go ahead and ask them to choose one of the topics on page 105 to research at home. Ask them to bring in their statistics for the writing class. Remind them to write down information about where they found the statistics and to choose reliable sources (review ideas from the *Study skills* sections of units 3 and 8).

Writing skill

Ask students to read the *Qualifying statistical data* box to find words that help describe trends. Ask them to say if the words show a big or small change. Once they have read the box, ask them to say what they think the word *qualifying* means from the context of what they have read (changing or modifying something slightly to make it more accurate).

Ask students to complete the sentences about the charts with the phrases for describing trends and adjectives and adverbs from the *Qualifying statistical data* box. Then check the answers with the class.

> **POSSIBLE ANSWERS**
> Chart a
> 1 remain steady; dip
> 2 remain constant; slight dip
> Chart b
> 1 slightly rise; suddenly surge; remain steady
> 2 slight increase; sharply rose; remained steady
> Chart c
> 1 dipped slightly; sudden spike; remain steady
> 2 steep increase; skyrocketed; remain steady

Grammar

Ask students to read the *Grammar* box to learn about the future progressive and why it is used.

1 Ask students to complete the sentences from *Career trends* with the correct form of the future progressive. Have them check their answers in the article before checking with the whole class.

> **ANSWERS**
> 1 will be including
> 2 will be uploading
> 3 will be using
> 4 will be providing
> 5 will be expanding

2 Ask students to work with a partner to discuss the questions. Point out before they start that they should focus on using the future progressive in their discussion, and circulate to check they are using it correctly.

WRITING TASK

The writing task requires students to do some research to find statistics to support their views. In the *Plan* section, a list of ideas for how to gather the information is given. The best source of information will vary according to which topic is chosen. Note that the first two, *Interviews* and *Surveys and questionnaires*, require students to do primary research. You may need to help students think of questions to ask, and decide who the best people are to ask in order to get the information sample they need, how many people to ask, and the best way to get the information they need (e.g. individual interviews, questionnaires that are sent out—the problem here is whether or not they would get them all back in time, an online survey tool, email). Whichever method they choose, they will need sufficient time to do the research.

Reports generally have subheadings. An example layout is shown in the notes for the *Write* section. Draw students' attention to the box that details the audience, context, and purpose of the writing task.

Brainstorm

1 Ask students to choose a topic that they are interested in and that they feel is changing.

2 Ask students to use a word map to brainstorm some of the reasons for the changes. You could put them into pairs to help each other generate ideas.

Plan

Ask students to firstly think about who they are writing their report for and why they want that person or people to know the information. Refer them to the ideas for gathering statistical data. Point out that interviews and surveys / questionnaires require them to do primary research—that is, they will have to design research questions and ask real people for their answers, then create their own graphs or charts from their data. Be sure to remind them to note down where they get their information from and to choose reliable sources (review the *Study skills* section of units 3 and 8).

Write

You could specify a layout for the report. For example:

Title:

Purpose / Aim of the report

The purpose / aim of this report is to …

Findings: description of the trend

X has been increasing … Y is growing rapidly …

(graphs and charts can be included in this section)

Predictions and conclusions (or recommendations, if applicable)

Because X will be -ing … I recommend …

References

Ask students to aim for 300–350 words. Have them include a separate page with references, or, if they did primary research, to include their questionnaire or survey questions.

Share, rewrite, and edit

Ask students to exchange their report with a partner. When students read their partner's report, they should focus on whether they can understand the report and the graphs and charts in it. Ask students to exchange their paragraphs with a partner. Encourage students to use the Peer review checklist on page 109 when they are evaluating their partner's paragraph. Ask them to feed back on what needs to be made clearer before the rewriting and editing stage. Ask students to rewrite and edit their reports. Encourage them to take into consideration their partner's feedback when rewriting.

Use the photocopiable unit assignment checklist on page 97 to assess the students' reports.

Extra research task

If you have enough time, you could do a group research project in which groups of students do both primary and secondary research. Each group would choose a topic and work together to create a questionnaire or survey. They would conduct the survey and find other information at the library or online to support their findings. They could either write up their report as a group or present their findings during a group presentation.

STUDY SKILLS Developing a portfolio

The term *portfolio* can have a lot of meanings, but here it means a collection of personal achievements including education, examples of work, reflections, and personal objectives. An e-portfolio is one you put up and maintain in order to allow easy access for potential employers, degree programs, or any other professional purpose. It can include links and videoed personal statements and can be used to illustrate technology skills. Both types of portfolios provide a platform for people to showcase their abilities and achievements.

If you have a portfolio, you could bring it in to show the students. Otherwise, pre-teach the term and ask students to skim the page for 20 seconds to find out what information they will learn about portfolios. Ask students to read the section *What is the purpose of a portfolio?* Ask them to discuss why they think a portfolio might be useful. Find out if anyone has a portfolio and, if so, what they include in it. Brainstorm some ideas for what students might put in a portfolio, then ask them to read the rest of the text.

Ask students to go through the list in the *What to put in your portfolio* section to brainstorm and discuss what personal information they could include for each. For example, in number 4, students could list any courses they have done, including the English course they are undertaking currently. Ask them to write down all the things they think they would be able to add to each section.

As a wrap-up to the course, ask students to write a personal statement (number 10). Not only are personal statements required for entrance into many colleges and universities, but they also provide an opportunity to reflect on goals, past experience, and personal strengths.

Encourage students to begin compiling either an online or paper-based portfolio. For online portfolios, you could direct students to sites such as wix.com, bigblackbag.com, or portfoliobox.net on which they can create an online portfolio, or you could ask them to search for some professional online portfolios.

Tomorrow

Since online portfolios can take such a myriad of forms, ask students to think about what kind of portfolio it is: professional or personal, and what kind of field the person might be in.

For more tips on writing personal statements, students could go to the UCAS website (ucas.ac.uk) which gives detailed instructions on writing a good personal (or mission) statement. Another good site is the Purdue Owl site: http://owl.english.purdue.edu/owl/resource/642/01/.

For examples of personal statements, go to http://www.studential.com/personalstatements/. Encourage students NOT to copy the style or content—employers and registrars read a lot of personal statements, so they should be personal and reflect the uniqueness of each individual.

Unit assignment

Student name: _____

Date: _____

Unit assignment: A paragraph about your identity

25 points: Excellent achievement. Student successfully fulfils the expectation for this part of the assignment with little or no room for improvement.

20 points: Good achievement. Student fulfils the expectation for this part of the assignment, but may have a few errors or need some improvement.

15 points: Satisfactory achievement. Student needs some work to fulfil the expectation for this part of the assignment, but shows some effort.

5 points: Poor achievement. Student does not fulfil the expectation for this part of the assignment.

	Met		Unmet		Comments
The paragraph is 125–150 words.					
	25 points	20 points	15 points	5 points	
The paragraph has a topic sentence which introduces the main idea.					
The sentences in the paragraph support the main idea of the topic sentence.					
The paragraph uses clauses with subordinating conjunctions.					
The paragraph has a concluding sentence.					

Total: _____ /100

Comments:

UNIT 2 DESIGN

Student name: _____

Date: _____

Unit assignment: The pros and cons of a design

25 points: Excellent achievement. Student successfully fulfils the expectation for this part of the assignment with little or no room for improvement.

20 points: Good achievement. Student fulfils the expectation for this part of the assignment, but may have a few errors or need some improvement.

15 points: Satisfactory achievement. Student needs some work to fulfil the expectation for this part of the assignment, but shows some effort.

5 points: Poor achievement. Student does not fulfil the expectation for this part of the assignment.

	Met		Unmet		Comments
Each paragraph is 150–200 words.					
	25 points	20 points	15 points	5 points	
The paragraphs are well-organized with topic and concluding sentences.					
The first paragraph describes the structure in detail.					
The second paragraph discusses the pros and cons of the design and suggests ideas for improving it.					
The language for introducing opposing ideas is correct. At least one non-defining relative clause is used correctly.					

Total: _____ /100

Comments:

UNIT 3 THOUGHT

Student name: _____

Date: _____

Unit assignment: A summary and a response paragraph

25 points: Excellent achievement. Student successfully fulfils the expectation for this part of the assignment with little or no room for improvement.

20 points: Good achievement. Student fulfils the expectation for this part of the assignment, but may have a few errors or need some improvement.

15 points: Satisfactory achievement. Student needs some work to fulfil the expectation for this part of the assignment, but shows some effort.

5 points: Poor achievement. Student does not fulfil the expectation for this part of the assignment.

	Met		Unmet		Comments
The summary paragraph is 65–90 words.					
The response paragraph is 120–150 words.					
	25 points	20 points	15 points	5 points	
The summary says what the reading is about (the topic).					
The summary includes key points and no details.					
The response includes opinions supported by examples.					
The response includes adverb clauses of reason and purpose.					

Total: _____ /100

Comments:

UNIT 4 FIRE

Student name: _____

Date: _____

Unit assignment: Narrative essay: A time when you faced danger

25 points: Excellent achievement. Student successfully fulfils the expectation for this part of the assignment with little or no room for improvement.

20 points: Good achievement. Student fulfils the expectation for this part of the assignment, but may have a few errors or need some improvement.

15 points: Satisfactory achievement. Student needs some work to fulfil the expectation for this part of the assignment, but shows some effort.

5 points: Poor achievement. Student does not fulfil the expectation for this part of the assignment.

	Met		Unmet		Comments
The narrative is 200–250 words.					
	25 points	20 points	15 points	5 points	
The narrative describes the sequence of events clearly.					
The narrative includes sensory details.					
The narrative includes stance markers.					
The narrative is well-structured with topic and concluding sentences.					

Total: _____ /100

Comments:

Unit assignment

UNIT 5 MOVEMENT

Student name: _____

Date: _____

Unit assignment: Response to an exam question

25 points: Excellent achievement. Student successfully fulfils the expectation for this part of the assignment with little or no room for improvement.

20 points: Good achievement. Student fulfils the expectation for this part of the assignment, but may have a few errors or need some improvement.

15 points: Satisfactory achievement. Student needs some work to fulfil the expectation for this part of the assignment, but shows some effort.

5 points: Poor achievement. Student does not fulfil the expectation for this part of the assignment.

	Met		Unmet		Comments
The paragraph is 150–175 words.					
	25 points	20 points	15 points	5 points	
The paragraph answers the exam question completely.					
The paragraph is well-structured with topic and concluding sentences.					
The paragraph uses several noun clauses with *that*.					
The paragraph uses a variety of sentence types.					

Total: _____ /100

Comments:

UNIT 6 DISEASE

Student name: _____

Date: _____

Unit assignment: Persuasive essay: A health recommendation

25 points: Excellent achievement. Student successfully fulfils the expectation for this part of the assignment with little or no room for improvement.

20 points: Good achievement. Student fulfils the expectation for this part of the assignment, but may have a few errors or need some improvement.

15 points: Satisfactory achievement. Student needs some work to fulfil the expectation for this part of the assignment, but shows some effort.

5 points: Poor achievement. Student does not fulfil the expectation for this part of the assignment.

	Met		Unmet		Comments
The essay is 250–300 words.					
	25 points	20 points	15 points	5 points	
The first paragraph describes the health issue and includes a thesis statement which explains the main point, opinion, and how it will be supported.					
The second paragraph gives reasons and examples to support the recommendations.					
The final paragraph concludes the essay by summarizing the issue and recommendations.					
Passive modals are used correctly.					

Total: _____ /100

Comments:

Unit assignment

Student name: _____

Date: _____

Unit assignment: Describing a challenging situation

25 points: Excellent achievement. Student successfully fulfils the expectation for this part of the assignment with little or no room for improvement.

20 points: Good achievement. Student fulfils the expectation for this part of the assignment, but may have a few errors or need some improvement.

15 points: Satisfactory achievement. Student needs some work to fulfil the expectation for this part of the assignment, but shows some effort.

5 points: Poor achievement. Student does not fulfil the expectation for this part of the assignment.

	Met		Unmet		Comments
The article is 300–375 words.					
	25 points	20 points	15 points	5 points	
The first paragraph describes the situation and what happened in detail. It is well organized with a topic and concluding sentence.					
The second paragraph describes what might have happened differently and how the dangerous situation could have been avoided. It includes a topic and concluding sentence.					
The final paragraph concludes with recommendations about precautions to take and what you should have with you. It has a topic and concluding sentence.					
Cause and effect and unreal conditionals in the past are used correctly.					

Total: _____ /100

Comments:

UNIT 8 DRIVE

Student name: _____

Date: _____

Unit assignment: A proposal

25 points: Excellent achievement. Student successfully fulfils the expectation for this part of the assignment with little or no room for improvement.

20 points: Good achievement. Student fulfils the expectation for this part of the assignment, but may have a few errors or need some improvement.

15 points: Satisfactory achievement. Student needs some work to fulfil the expectation for this part of the assignment, but shows some effort.

5 points: Poor achievement. Student does not fulfil the expectation for this part of the assignment.

	Met		Unmet		Comments
The proposal is 300–350 words.					
	25 points	20 points	15 points	5 points	
The proposal contains an effective hook to grab the reader's attention.					
The proposal clearly details the plan and who it will help.					
The proposal gives sound examples and details to convince the reader of the positive effects of the project.					
The proposal gives sound details about the needs for the project and the reason for these requests.					

Total: _____ /100

Comments:

Unit assignment

Student name: _____

Date: _____

Unit assignment: A descriptive anecdote

25 points: Excellent achievement. Student successfully fulfils the expectation for this part of the assignment with little or no room for improvement.

20 points: Good achievement. Student fulfils the expectation for this part of the assignment, but may have a few errors or need some improvement.

15 points: Satisfactory achievement. Student needs some work to fulfil the expectation for this part of the assignment, but shows some effort.

5 points: Poor achievement. Student does not fulfil the expectation for this part of the assignment.

	Met		Unmet		Comments
The anecdote is 250–300 words.					
	25 points	20 points	15 points	5 points	
The anecdote uses a variety of descriptive adjectives correctly.					
The anecdote has at least one effective simile or metaphor.					
The anecdote uses a variety of sentence types including at least one cleft sentence.					
The anecdote is well-organized so that the story is easy to follow and understand.					

Total: _____ /100

Comments:

Skillful Level 3 Reading & Writing Teacher's Book.
This page is photocopiable, but all copies must be complete pages.
Copyright © Macmillan Publishers Limited 2013.

UNIT 10 TOMORROW

Student name: _____

Date: _____

Unit assignment: A report on a current trend

25 points: Excellent achievement. Student successfully fulfils the expectation for this part of the assignment with little or no room for improvement.

20 points: Good achievement. Student fulfils the expectation for this part of the assignment, but may have a few errors or need some improvement.

15 points: Satisfactory achievement. Student needs some work to fulfil the expectation for this part of the assignment, but shows some effort.

5 points: Poor achievement. Student does not fulfil the expectation for this part of the assignment.

	Met		Unmet		Comments
The report is 300–350 words.					
	25 points	20 points	15 points	5 points	
The report describes the trend and its effects in detail.					
The report includes graphs, charts, or tables.					
The report concludes with a prediction for how the trend will continue in the future and recommendations if applicable.					
The report uses trend language effectively and uses the future progressive where possible.					

Total: _____ /100

Comments:

UNIT 1 Identity

Vocabulary preview

1

1 e 2 a 3 h 4 c 5 b 6 g 7 f 8 d

READING 1 Discuss it online

Global reading

Possible answers:

1 The instructor wants to have students think about their own identity and relate it to the three aspects of identity before class.
2 He had a bad knee injury and had to quit the soccer team.
3 Ali writes about the values of hard work and competition.
4 During high school, Paul wasn't close with his parents, and his friends influenced him in bad ways.
5 His new friends understand his family background and his values.
6 Ali would probably agree, because even when he had to give up his chosen identity (soccer player), he was still the same person inside.

Close reading

1 The instructor defines given identity, chosen identity, and core identity.
2 The instructor gives examples for each to help define the term.
3 It is a chosen identity.
4 Answers will vary.

READING 2 Sports fans and identity

Global reading

a 3 b 5 c 1 d 4 e X f 2

Close reading

1

1 Individual identity consists of <u>many things, including our gender, personality, abilities, and social groups.</u>
2 According to social identity theory, <u>we naturally categorize people into groups.</u>
3 Self-esteem means <u>how we feel about ourselves.</u>

2

1 T
2 F (The groups we belong to <u>do</u> influence our self-esteem.)
3 F (Henri Tajfel and John Turner wrote about social identity in sports.)
4 F (Researchers found that fans use different pronouns to talk about their team, depending on if the team won or lost.)
5 T

Vocabulary skill

1

Noun	Verb	Adjective
choice	choose	chosen
concern	concern	concerned
identity	identify	identifiable
struggle	struggle	struggling
trust	trust	trustworthy

1 identifiable
2 choices
3 chose
4 concerned
5 trustworthy
6 struggles

2

1 What are you <u>concerned</u> about at the moment?
2 Do you have more <u>confidence</u> with reading or listening?
3 Do you find it easy to make <u>choices</u>?

Writing skill

1

1
a Social psychologists suggest that we have three basic types of identity.
b three
c listing organization
d No, it doesn't.

2
a When I started high school, I thought that I knew exactly who I was and where I was headed.
b time order organization
c Yes, it does.

2

Student's own answers

WRITING A paragraph about your identity

Grammar

1

1 before
2 Before
3 Whenever
4 although
5 if
6 Even though

2

1 ✗ I didn't understand the theory in physics class.
2 ✗ Although / Even though / After / Because / Since I had many struggles during my first semester, the second semester seemed much easier.
3 ✗ He didn't have much self-confidence because / since he had failed the course twice already.
4 ✓
5 ✗ She was extremely beautiful.
6 ✗ If / When their favorite coach is fired, the fans will be very upset.

WRITING TASK

Topic sentence: There are three different aspects that define my identity: my ____ identity, ___ identity, and ___ identity.
Concluding sentence: Of the three aspects of identity, for me my ____ identity is the most important right now.
Subordinating coordinator: I enjoy these groups <u>because</u> …

UNIT 2 Design

Vocabulary preview

1 iconic
2 feat
3 devise
4 dilemma
5 eyesore
6 opponents
7 landmarks
8 priority
9 Construction

READING 1 The Metropol Parasol

Global reading

1

The Metropol Parasol is a public community center in Seville, Spain. It includes shops, restaurants, and cafés, and a museum that exhibits Roman ruins.

2

1 name of a place (scan for capital letters)
2 name of a person (scan for capital letters)
3 dates and numbers (scan for numbers)
4 numbers (scan for numbers)
5 signal words and phrases (scan for *upper level*)

3

1 in Seville, Spain
2 German architect, Jürgen Mayer H.
3 seven years
4 90 million euros
5 a panorama deck

Close reading

1 F (The construction site was originally planned as a parking garage.)
2 T
3 T
4 T
5 T

READING 2 Designing solutions

Global reading

1

Name of project	Location	Year started	Reasons for project
1 New Valley Project	Western Desert, Egypt	1997	to turn area of desert into livable farmland, help solve overcrowding problems
2 Venice Tide Barrier Project	Venice, Italy	2003	to help stop frequent flooding in the city, protect historical landmarks

2

1 d 2 c 3 f 4 b 5 a 6 e

Close reading

1 population growth, climate change, and aging urban infrastructures
2 $436 million
3 1.2 million cubic meters per hour
4 25%
5 as much as 23 centimeters
6 28 meters high, 20 meters wide

Vocabulary skill

1 overflows
2 overconfident
3 overslept
4 overreacted
5 overestimated
6 overcrowding
7 overdone
8 overeat

WRITING The pros and cons of a design

Writing skill

1 The bridge is modern and attractive. However, there are many safety concerns.

2 Although the city needed a new hotel, the building is ugly and won't help attract tourists.

3 Whereas many people like modern, futuristic design, I prefer traditional architecture.

4 The Sky Mall isn't conveniently located. On the other hand, it has amazing views from the rooftop garden.

5 The parking lot may help local businesses. Nevertheless, it will destroy a natural wildlife habitat.

Grammar

1

1 City Hall, which houses the mayor's office, has a large golden dome on the top.

2 My cousin Casey, who works for a design firm, is one of my favorite relatives.

3 The new student center has a large outdoor area, which is a great place to eat lunch.

4 Last month I saw Jim Stafford, who was a friend from my university days.

5 We saw a lot of iconic buildings on our trip to India. We even got to watch the sunset over the Taj Mahal, which was incredibly romantic.

6 The old school on West Street, which closed last year, was built in 1792.

2

Students' own answers

WRITING TASK

Brainstorm

1

Transitions:

While the new complex offers lots of state-of-the-art equipment inside, the exterior appears too traditional and rather uninteresting, in my opinion.

However, there are no facilities for sports such as soccer or baseball, which are best played outdoors.

Despite these minor design issues, the Shankman Sports Complex is certain to be a busy place year round.

Non-defining relative clauses:

The new Shankman Sports Complex, which was completed in March 2012, is a brand new sports facility.

The entrance includes some welcoming decorative features, such as a fountain and a statue of the founder, Tom Shankman, who was a minor-league baseball player.

However, there are no facilities for sports such as soccer or baseball, which are best played outdoors.

STUDY SKILLS Editing and proofreading strategies

Scenario

While Ramon was doing the right thing in re-reading his work and checking for errors before handing it in, he needed a better system to help him do a more thorough check. It can be especially difficult to see one's own errors in writing. Becoming familiar with common mistakes, using an editing checklist, and asking a peer to review are helpful habits.

UNIT 3 Thought

Vocabulary preview

1 Evidence
2 study
3 accuracy
4 performance
5 efficiency
6 concentrate
7 expand
8 challenge

READING 1 Is your memory online?

Global reading

2

1 the Internet
2 information
3 experiments
4 different
5 research

Close reading

1 Psychologist at Columbia University conducted ~~3~~ 4 experiments
   Aim: How is the Internet changing ~~students~~ memory?

2 Experiment: people typed words into a computer
   1st group: knew computer would~~n't~~ save information
   2nd group: knew computer ~~would~~ wouldn't save information
   Result: ~~1st~~ 2nd group remembered the info better

3 Experiment: gave people info to remember and where to find the folder with the information on the computer
   Result: Later, people remembered the location of the info better than the ~~name of the folder~~ facts

4 Transactive memory: we ~~forget~~ remember where to find the information we need

5 Conclusion: because of the Internet, our transactive memory is becoming ~~weaker~~ stronger.

READING 2 How does the brain multitask?

Global reading

1

1 F 2 T 3 F 4 F

2

1 electronic media
2 to view the brain in action

Close reading

1

1 One group were given one task, but the other group were given two tasks to do.

2 It showed that the brain only works on one task at a time.

3 They used MRI images to monitor brain activity during the tasks.

4 It takes longer to complete each task and more mistakes are made.

5 These tasks require less concentration.

2

Possible answers:

1 describes things that use technology such as laptops, cell phones, and computers

2 television, radio, Internet, etc. (the opposite of "print media")

---

3 the area in the front of the brain responsible for problem solving, decision making, planning, and emotions.

4 at the same time
5 going from one to another
6 reduces
7 a restriction
8 the words of a song

Vocabulary skill

1

Possible answers:

1 conducted; analyzed
2 conducted; analyzed
3 adopted; addressed
4 analyzed; conducted
5 analyze
6 address; adopting

2

Student's own answers

WRITING A summary and a response paragraph

Writing skill

1

1 Is your memory online?
2 memory
3 experiments
4 remember
5 memories

2

1 sentence 1, memory

2 Possible answers include: memory, research, information, transactive memories, experiments, Internet

3 People are developing strong transactive memories.

4 The article *Is your memory online?* discusses research that shows that people are becoming better at remembering where to find information online, but that it isn't clear if people's memories are becoming weaker.

3

Possible answer:

In the article *How does the brain multitask?*, the author explains what multitasking is and discusses recent research about what happens in the brain while we multitask. Research shows that the brain does not actually do two things at the same time, but rather switches quickly between tasks. The brain uses its working memory to store information on one task while switching to the second task. Working on more than two tasks at a time leads to more mistakes. Experts say that it is better to concentrate on one task and do it efficiently.

Grammar

1

1 so that
2 Because / Since / As
3 because / since / as / due to the fact that
4 because / since / as / due to the fact that
5 in order to

2

Possible answers:

1 As I hope to have a career in international business, it's important for me to be fluent in English.

2 I use the Internet in order to do online research for my classes, and to communicate with friends and family.

3 Sometimes I go to the library and set a time for myself to work without stopping so that I can focus on my studies.

4 While I am doing my homework on the computer, I often have a chat window open and my email open so that I can get messages from my friends. Since it is more fun and easier to socialize than to study, I often end up wasting my time chatting with friends rather than getting my schoolwork finished.

5 I often have good ideas in the early morning, before my day gets started. It's a quiet time of day, and my mind is more relaxed so that it is more open to good ideas. I also get good ideas when I am walking because I allow my mind to wander.

WRITING TASK

Brainstorm

1

He felt much calmer, his concentration was better, and he seemed to be more creative in solving problems.

Adverb clause of reason: In order to examine how multitasking may cause stress in my own life, I decided to try the author's no-multitasking experiment.

Adverb clause of purpose: It would be interesting do set up a school experiment so that we could learn how other students experience a few days of no multitasking.

UNIT 4 Fire

Discussion point

1
1 b 2 d 3 a 4 c

Vocabulary preview
1 a 2 b 3 b 4 a 5 a 6 a 7 a 8 a

READING 1 Feeling the heat

Global reading

1

Possible answers:

1 Most people run away from danger; however, firefighters are an exception.

2 Firefighters not only put out fires; they also help educate people in the community about how to prevent them.

3 Being a firefighter requires physical fitness, knowledge of the science of fire, and the ability to stay calm under stress.

4 Fighting fires can be scary, and some situations are very stressful, but it's a rewarding job.

2

b (The summary is shorter than the original paragraph, expresses the main points using different words, and does not include too many details.)

Close reading

1 a range of situations

2 an interview and two tests

---

3 to make decisions quickly

4 are afraid when they see firefighters

5 sometimes feels afraid

READING 2 Fire in the sky

Global reading

Possible answer:

Fireworks, also called pyrotechnics, have been used as a form of entertainment for centuries. The first firecrackers were made from bamboo in China around 200 BCE.

Later, between 600–900 CE, Chinese chemists began experimenting with making firecrackers by putting different types of chemicals into tubes.

In 1292, Marco Polo introduced fireworks to Italy.

During the Renaissance, Italians began to make true pyrotechnics. Word spread to other countries, and fireworks became a popular form of entertainment.

By the 1700s in England, fireworks displays became big public events.

Today, fireworks displays may include between 40 and 50 thousand fireworks. They are operated by highly trained professionals using computers.

Close reading
1 f 2 b 3 d 4 a 5 e 6 c

Vocabulary skill

1

We've got to try to stop fires before they even start.

You've got to be in excellent physical condition.

You've got to pass a challenging written exam.

We've got to understand the science of fire.

We've got to assess the situation quickly.

Honestly, I've got to admit that I was nervous.

2
1 've got to   4 've got to
2 's got to   5 've got to
3 've got to

WRITING Narrative essay: A time when you faced danger

Writing skill
1 bright, sunny   6 steep, narrow
2 fresh, clean-smelling 7 rough and rocky
3 birds singing   8 snap
4 colorful   9 sharp pain
5 pinkish orange

Grammar skill

1
1 Naturally   4 Fortunately
2 Honestly   5 Amazingly
3 Unfortunately

2
1 Naturally / Obviously

2 Surprisingly / Amazingly / Thankfully / Fortunately

3 Surprisingly / Shockingly / Amazingly / Thankfully / Fortunately / Luckily

4 Thankfully / Fortunately

5 Thankfully / Fortunately / Luckily

UNIT 5 Movement

Vocabulary preview
1 d 2 c 3 a 4 b 5 f 6 h 7 g 8 e

READING 1 Invasive species you should know

Global reading

2 a ALBs have been carried by cars and trucks in the U.S.

3 b Red imported fire ants came to the U.S. from South America.

5 c It's important to learn to recognize invasive species.

1 d Many invasive species are introduced into new habitats every year as a result of global trade.

4 e RIFAs can move their colonies quickly and easily.

Close reading
1 a 2 b 3 a 4 b 5 a

Developing critical thinking

1

Asian longhorned beetle	Red imported fire ants
wooden crates on ships	soil in ships
not very easily	easily
it doesn't	attacks people
yes, but very expensive	no

2

Red imported fire ants are the most problematic because they can attack people and sting. They can also move around easily and multiply quickly, and are impossible to get rid of.

READING 2 How do animals navigate?

Global reading

2
1 d 2 a 3 e 4 b 5 f 6 c

7 *Possible answer:* If they lose contact with the infrasound waves while they're flying over the ocean, pigeons get lost. / The loud sound of the airplane made them lose their way.

Close reading

	Where do they navigate (to/from)?	How do they navigate?
1 Sea turtles	from place of birth to other areas for food to birthplace to lay eggs	They use a magnetic map, mostly, as well as a sense of smell and sight.
2 Homing pigeons	from an unfamiliar location to their home nest	They use a magnetic map, sight, smell, infrasound, and they fly over highways.
3 Fruit bats	from their caves to trees	They use visual clues such as lights and hills, magnetic fields, and smell.

Vocabulary skill

1

1 at	3 on	5 in	7 on
2 to	4 out	6 by	8 of

2

1 drawn back to	4 figure out
2 puzzled by	5 in search of
3 rely on	6 concentrating on

WRITING Response to an exam question

Writing skill
Possible answers:

1 He's not fluent in English, but / though he's adept at making himself understood. / Although he's not fluent in English, he's adept at making himself understood.
2 My final destination is Italy, but / although I have to fly to Zurich first.
3 The typhoon was devastating, and many people lost their homes.
4 When / If an animal's habitat is destroyed by human activity, it must search for a new area.
5 Because Costa Rica is famous for its natural beauty and unspoiled environment, recently it has become a very popular spot for foreign tourists.

2
Possible answer:

Some people can easily find their way in an unfamiliar place, while other people seem to get lost in their own towns. Recent studies have found genetic connections to people's ability to navigate, which may explain why some people are skillful at navigating. Some people are easily disoriented and get lost easily. Studies show that good navigators use landmarks and streets to orient themselves. They use visual geometry. In their heads, they visualize their location in relation to things they see around them. Researchers have found that people with a rare genetic disease can't visually orient themselves. Experts now believe that navigational skills are inherited and that some people lack certain navigation genes.

Grammar

1

1 It is clear that many animals travel great distances during migration.
2 It is a fact that animal migration is often interrupted by human activities.
3 It is obvious that each year many animals must migrate to find fresh sources of food.
4 It was widely believed that migrating nocturnal bats were blown to the island of Hawaii in a storm.
5 It has been shown that oil pipelines interrupt the migration routes of caribou in Canada.
6 It is a fact that each year 5 billion birds migrate from North to Central and South America. / It is a fact that 5 billion birds migrate from North to Central and South America each year.
7 It has been reported that some migrating birds can fly without stopping for 50 to 60 hours.

2
Students' own answers

WRITING TASK

Brainstorm

1

1 Five pieces of information should be in the answer. The writer didn't include information about why the habitat is suitable.
2 The kudzu is an invasive species of plant that has spread …
   The problem was that it grew too fast.
3 There is good variety. There are two very short sentences. (*The problem was that it grew too fast. It spread out of control.*)

STUDY SKILLS Strategies for writing timed essays

Scenario

This is what Jun Ho is doing right: he includes examples or details to support his opinion; he leaves time at the end to check his spelling and grammar. This is what he is doing wrong: he doesn't carefully review the exam question; he starts writing his answer without gathering and organizing his main idea and support; he writes without stopping, thinking that writing more is better than writing well.

UNIT 6 Disease

Vocabulary preview

1 precise	5 diagnosis
2 resolve	6 symptoms
3 widespread	7 genetic
4 application	8 disorders

READING 1 Long-distance care

Global reading
A definition of telesurgery:
The doctor is not in the operating room, using a robot and a computer to perform the surgery.
History:
First performed in 2001: Dr. Jacques Marescaux in New York City performed gall bladder operation on a woman in France.
Advantages:
can be used in places where access to medical care is limited, or travel is difficult; accuracy
The future of telesurgery:
training surgeons in developing countries, treating injured soldiers on battlefield, conducting surgical procedures in space

Close reading
Possible answers:

1 from a hospital far away, without a surgeon in the operating room
2 the Internet and fiber-optic cables
3 touched by the surgeon's hands
4 where access to medical care may be limited
5 more accurate
6 for injured soldiers on the battlefield, or in space

READING 2 Do we know too much?

Global reading

1 patients who are displaying symptoms of diseases or who have already been diagnosed with certain diseases
2 four: newborn screening, diagnostic testing, carrier testing, and predictive testing
3 hair or tissue from inside a person's mouth
4 researching a family history and identifying criminals

Close reading
1 O 2 F 3 O 4 O 5 F 6 F

Vocabulary skill

1
1 c 2 d 3 a 4 b 5 f 6 g 7 e 8 h

2

1 cerebral	5 optician
2 cardiologist	6 autobiography
3 antianxiety	7 psychoanalyst
4 ambiguous	8 neurological

WRITING Persuasive essay: A health recommendation

Writing skill

1
b

2
3 Many health problems can be avoided if people get enough sleep and take steps to reduce stress.
5 Older adults should consider the health benefits of switching to a vegetarian diet, including weight loss and a lower risk of heart disease.
6 The most important step in preventing disease is for parents to encourage their children to eat more fresh fruits and vegetables, and fewer sugary, fatty junk foods.

3
Possible answers:

1 People should choose not to have genetic testing because the tests cause unnecessary stress, are too costly, and have poor accuracy rates.
2 People can reduce their risk of heart problems if they avoid stress, get enough rest, and exercise regularly.
4 Employers can offer insurance to both full and part-time employees, if they allow part-time employees to pay a percentage of the cost or select lower-cost insurance plans.
7 Insurance companies should cover telesurgery because it has better accuracy and lower risk of infection than traditional surgery.
8 A vegetarian diet can help people lose weight and improve health; however if they do not follow certain guidelines, health problems can actually arise.

Grammar

1

1 Possibility	4 Possibility
2 Ability	5 Ability
3 Advice	

2
1 All diseases might be prevented someday.
2 The risks of an inactive lifestyle should be considered.
3 Stress can be reduced if people make time to do the things they enjoy.
4 Good health habits can be learned from an early age.
5 Genetic tests should only be taken for treatable diseases.
6 A doctor should be consulted about any health concerns.
7 Memory in older people can be improved through walking.

STUDY SKILLS Participating in online discussion boards

Scenario
At first, Fatima did not read the instructor's guidelines for online discussion boards. This could have prevented the embarrassing situation. While her response to her classmate was direct, the style she used was too casual, and she did not support her opinion with reasons or examples.

UNIT 7 Survival

Vocabulary preview
1 a 2 b 3 a 4 a 5 b 6 b 7 a 8 b

READING 1 *Adrift:* A book report

Global reading

1
1 *Adrift: Seventy-Six Days Lost at Sea*, Steven Callahan, 1986
2 non-fiction
3 The writer likes to read about true-life survival stories.
4 The story is about a sailor who survives in an inflatable raft for 76 days. It takes place on the Atlantic Ocean.
5 Yes, the writer likes the book because the reader can experience the author's struggles.
6 *Students' own answers*

2
Possible answer:
Adrift, by Steven Callahan, is a true story of a man's struggle to survive at sea after his sailboat sinks. The book describes his struggles, both physical and mental, to survive alone on the Atlantic Ocean for 76 days.

Close reading

1
1 real
2 *Adrift*
3 survival
4 England
5 experienced
6 prepared
7 large object
8 sinks
9 76
10 inflatable raft
11 salt
12 drinking
13 food
14 exercise

Possible answers:
Paragraph 4
reader experiences Callahan's struggle
suffers from hunger, thirst, and weather
his self-control and problem-solving help him survive
Paragraph 5
author's writing style brings the book alive
strength of spirit and knowledge help him survive
reading the book is unforgettable

READING 2 A semester on ice

Before you read
1 continent
2 South
3 summer; always
4 the U.S.
5 dangerous

Global reading

1
1 Hypothermia is when the body temperature drops to 35°C (95°F) or below, leading to a chain of events that can result in death.
2 lots of clothing, adequate shelter from the weather and moisture, appropriate and sufficient food, and water
3 Questions 2, 3, and 5 are answered in the blog.
4 *Possible answer:* Because the conditions are so treacherous, and they may not have communication, people need to know how to stay safe and warm.

Close reading
1 f 2 g 3 e 4 d 5 c 6 a 7 b

Developing critical thinking

1
Possible answers:
1 All types of research are done in Antarctica. It's important because scientists can study subjects under very extreme weather conditions, and they can see the effects of weather and the changing climate on animals and resources in Antarctica.
2 He learned about conducting important research in a very remote area. In addition, he will learn about team work, about working in a situation where you cannot easily get replacement parts or assistance, and about a unique part of the world. His unusual experience will help him stand out when he applies for a job.

2

Keys for survival	Callahan's situation
clothing and insulation	I can infer that his clothing didn't protect him from the sun, heat, cold, and moisture.
shelter	He didn't have protection from the sun or water, or the cold at night.
sufficient food	He didn't have food, but it says that he had a spear for fishing. He must have caught fish.
water	He didn't have enough drinking water, but he was able to devise a still to convert salt water to drinking water.

Vocabulary skill

1
1 inappropriate
2 uncertain
3 unconscious
4 inconvenient
5 independent
6 inexperienced
7 unfortunate
8 unintelligent
9 illegal
10 immature
11 unnecessary
12 imperfect
13 impractical
14 imprecise
15 insufficient
16 irresistible

2
1 popular
2 uninhabited
3 unbelievable
4 unusual
5 intelligent / independent
6 independent / intelligent
7 inappropriate
8 irresistible

WRITING Describing a challenging situation

Writing skill

1
1 C lack of insulation / E loss of body heat
2 E knew how to stay warm in snowstorm / C took a survival course
3 C eating high-energy food / E the body can generate energy
4 C suffering early hypothermia / E the person becomes confused
5 E dressed him in warm, dry clothing / C felt extremely cold
6 C sweating / E skin feels wet and cold

2
1 A result of
2 As a consequence of
3 enables; creates the skin to feel
4 produces
5 Because of
6 Therefore

3
Possible answers:
1 Walking in the hot sun made me very dehydrated.
2 As a consequence of the fog / it becoming foggy, I got lost in the mountains.
3 Not getting enough sleep can cause people to drive unsafely.
4 We were wearing fluorescent clothing. Therefore, the lifeboat crew saw us very easily.
5 The glow from my cell phone enabled me to find my way through the cave.

Grammar

1
1 hadn't sunk; might / would have been
2 hadn't known; couldn't have estimated
3 would have lost; hadn't exercised
4 would have died; hadn't devised
5 hadn't had; wouldn't have had
6 hadn't maintained; might / would have given up

2
Possible answers:
1 If I hadn't jumped out of the way, he would have hit me.
2 If I had reviewed the vocabulary, I would have done better.
3 If I had carefully read my essay before I handed it in, I could have deleted some information.

4 If he hadn't fallen, he wouldn't have broken the chair. If the chair hadn't broken, it wouldn't have bumped the lamp. If he hadn't fallen, he wouldn't have broken his wrist.

5 If it had been windy, I would have been more nervous about my first sailing lesson.

WRITING TASK

Brainstorm

1

Thesis statement:

After surviving my own treacherous driving experience in the desert, I've learned that driving across the desert in hot weather requires careful planning and preparation.

Cause and effect statements:

Because you will be using your air conditioner to cool the interior of the car, you will be using more gas.

You will need to drink more water than usual due to the extreme heat.

UNIT 8 Drive

Vocabulary preview

1 a 2 b 3 b 4 b 5 a 6 a 7 b 8 b

READING 1 Making a difference

Global reading

Possible answers:

1 He grew up in rural Malawi, and lived with his parents and seven sisters in a small clay house without electricity or running water. He had to work on the family farm and study. Life was hard.

2 He had to quit school when he was 13. He wasn't ready to give up his education. He read books from the local library.

3 He saw a picture of a windmill in a library book and began to collect materials. He endured many challenges and failures, but his ambition and determination helped him to continue until he achieved it.

4 With the help of international supporters, his village has clean water, solar lights, and electric power. He was invited to study at Dartmouth College. He travels around the world giving talks.

Close reading

1 work and study
2 kerosene oil is expensive
3 did not get any rain
4 a picture in a library book
5 finally completed his first windmill
6 has clean water, solar powered lighting, and electric power

READING 2 Most likely to succeed

Global reading

1 interview, scholarly journal, popular journal, website

2 interview—quote, advice
scholarly journal—information about a research study and its results
popular journal—quote, examples and terms

website—quote, advice, tips, examples

3 *Students' own answers*

Close reading

1 goals
2 are persistent
3 teach them ambition
4 have financial stress
5 doing more activities outside of school
6 appreciate our friends and family

Vocabulary skill

1

a straight-A student
b go-getter
c The grass is always greener on the other side.
d the rat race
e at any cost
f the social ladder

2

1 climb the social ladder
2 straight-A student
3 go-getter
4 the rat race
5 The grass is always greener on the other side.
6 at any cost

3

make it to the top (to be very successful);
you'll go far (to do very well in life, to achieve)

WRITING A proposal

Writing skill

1

A strong statement

Grammar

1

Making a difference: even harder, much better
Most likely to succeed: significantly higher, much higher

2

Students' own answers

STUDY SKILLS Selecting and evaluating online sources

Scenario

Possible answer:

These days, the Internet is the most popular method used for research. Mariana was right to begin with a search term or question. However, when the list of websites opens, she clicks on the site at the top of the list and begins taking notes immediately. Before using a website for research, she should scan its content and make sure it contains what she is looking for. It's best to scan a number of websites to see which ones offer the most useful information. Then, she should check the validity of the sites, making sure they are accurate, use citations, and are written by reliable sources.

UNIT 9 Sound

Vocabulary preview

1 affected   5 roar
2 distinguish   6 confused
3 audible   7 swept
4 ceased   8 troubled

READING 1 *The Secret Garden*: An excerpt

Global reading

1

1 They are inside a house, sitting by a fire.
2 Mary things the sound has come from inside the house, down one of the long corridors.
3 It was probably the wind.
4 The author shows letters missing from words with apostrophes. The author quotes Martha as saying *wutherin'* instead of *wuthering*, and *on th' moor an' wailin'* instead of *on the moor and wailing*.

2

Possible answers:

mysterious: 'It must mean that hollow, shuddering sort of roar which rushed round and round the house, as if the giant no one could see were buffeting it and beating at the walls and windows to try to break in.' / 'It was a curious sound—it seemed almost as if a child were crying somewhere.'

puzzled: 'It was a curious sound—it seemed almost as if a child were crying somewhere.'

scary: It must mean that hollow, shuddering sort of roar which rushed round and round the house, as if the giant no one could see were buffeting it and beating at the walls and windows to try to break in.'

suspicious: 'There!' said Mary. 'I told you so! It is someone crying—and it isn't a grown-up person.' / 'She did not believe she was speaking the truth.'

Close reading

1 f 2 e 3 g 4 a 5 b 6 c 7 d

Developing critical thinking

Possible answers:

1 The sound could be a child, or an animal, or just Mary's imagination. Martha may know a secret that she cannot tell Mary.

2 *Students' own answers*

READING 2 The loudest sound you've never heard

Global reading

1

1 The tone is academic and formal.
2 The purpose of this article is to inform, not to entertain like a story. Therefore, the author does not use language to create a mood. It is a science article (i.e. non-fiction).

2

5 Infrasound—heard by animals
3 Can be created by many natural events
6 How infrasound affects humans
X Can create health problems in humans
2 Discovery of infrasound
4 Travels through earth and ocean; can be measured
X Best methods for measuring sound
1 Infrasound—less than 20 hertz; very low

Close reading

1

1 F (Scientists can measure sounds that are less than 20 hertz.)

ANSWER KEY   103

2 F (The Krakatoa Volcano erupted in Indonesia.)

3 T

4 F (Before a volcano erupts, there is a great increase in infrasound.)

5 T

6 T

7 F (Experiments have shown that about 22% of people may be affected by infrasound.)

2

1 Infrasound is a sound that human cannot hear, but can be measured at 20 hertz or less.

2 It broke windows hundreds of miles away and affected barometers around the world.

3 Volcanoes, earthquakes, ocean storms, hurricanes, auroras, and air turbulence.

4 It increases in frequency and power.

5 Elephants use infrasound to communicate with other elephants.

6 It can make them feel uneasy.

Developing critical thinking
Possible answers:

1

1 Pros of hearing infrasound
We could hear infrasounds made by animals.
We might be able to predict volcanoes, hurricanes, or storms.
We could use it for communication.
It could enhance music concerts.
Cons of hearing infrasound
The additional noise would be distracting.
It might make many people nervous.
It might block other important sounds.
We might not be able to distinguish the source of the sound.

Vocabulary skill

1

1 round (sight), juicy (taste)

2 damp (touch), noisy (sound)

3 red (sight), friendly (sight or possibly sound)

4 dark (sight), dusty (touch or sight)

5 delicious (taste), green (sight)

2
Possible answers:

1 shrill / deafening

2 icy

3 damp

4 golden / bright

5 warm / soft

6 fragrant / delicious

7 soft / muffled

Writing skill

1

1 The wind is a giant.

2 The sound was like a child crying.

2
Possible answers:

1 the river

2 the sound of the water

3 high

4 it were a train whistle

5 noise

6 a person

7 a train

8 hard to hear

9 real

Grammar

1

1 C What he did was measure the low sound frequencies.

2 ✓

3 C What the children love is playing in the water.

4 ✓

5 ✓

6 C What they do is conduct experiments with infrasound.

2

1 What they decided to do was soundproof the music studio.

2 What I need to do is interview people who work with deaf people for my project.

3 What they want to discuss is solutions to the problems of noise pollution

4 What I felt upset about was that he wasn't listening to what I said.

5 What she always asks for is the quietest room in the hotel.

6 What I love is the sound of waves crashing on the shore.

3
Students' own answers

STUDY SKILLS Using the thesaurus

Scenario
Possible answer:

This is what Kumar is doing right: he is sometimes using the dictionary. This is what Kumar is doing wrong: he is not using an English–English dictionary, which would offer more possible word choices; he is not using a thesaurus to find words that may more concisely convey what he means.

UNIT 10 Tomorrow

Vocabulary preview

1 a 2 a 3 b 4 c 5 a 6 a

READING 1 Global graduates

Before you read
There is an increase in the number of students graduating from university.
Denmark and Portugal show the greatest shifts.

Global reading

1 The article discusses trends in graduation rates and international education.

2 According to the article, there has been an increase in the numbers of students graduating from university.

3 Countries around the world are expanding universities and trying to attract more international students.

4 The goals of these countries include bettering their financial situations and attracting talented people to help them compete with other countries.

5 A possible result of these trends is that foreign relations may improve.

Close reading

1 F (the attitude is optimistic: swelling tide, better still, more peaceful tomorrow, wonderful opportunities, lasting positive effects)

2 F (As expected ...)

3 T (it's clear a college education ... is becoming more a necessity than a luxury)

4 T (an entire 'Education City', boasting eight international university campuses, all in just one 14 square kilometer area)

5 F (Contrary to past limitations ...)

READING 2 Career trends

Global reading

1 It is an organization's "white paper" / report about a conference. Its purpose is to report findings after a conference discussion about professional hiring practices.

2 university students, job seekers, companies

3 Job seekers will use more technology to make their résumés stand out. Employers will be using social networking sites more frequently to recruit and check out prospective employees.

4 *Students' own answers*

Close reading

1 search for available jobs, and find employers and their company profiles

2 submit their résumé to a recruiter

3 walk-ins and career fairs

4 a good résumé, which summarizes the applicant's experience and highlights their most valuable skills

5 health and medical

6 It's approximately 11 times slower.

Vocabulary skill

1

| 1 D | 3 D | 5 U | 7 D | 9 U |
| 2 D | 4 D | 6 U | 8 U | 10 U |

2
Chart 1: spiked; dipped; skyrocketed
Chart 2: decline; grow; increase
Chart 3: decline; dive; rising
Chart 4: surged; rise; an increase

3
Answers will vary.

WRITING A report on a current trend

Writing skill
Possible answers:
Chart a
1 remain steady; dip
2 remain constant; slight dip
Chart b
1 slightly rise; suddenly surge; remain steady
2 slight increase; sharply rose; remained steady
Chart c
1 dipped slightly; sudden spike; remain steady
2 steep increase; skyrocketed; remain steady

Grammar

1

1 will be including

2 will be uploading

3 will be using

4 will be providing

5 will be expanding